DISCARD

When France Fell

By the same Author:

When
France
Fell

by H. J. GREENWALL

LONDON · ALLAN WINGATE

First Published 1958
by Allan Wingate (Publishers) Ltd
12 Beauchamp Place, London S.W.3

Made and Printed in Great Britain
by the Ditchling Press Ltd
Ditchling, Hassocks, Sussex

First Published June 1958

Foreword

A NUMBER OF YEARS have gone sailing by since I published my autobiography: *I Hate Tomorrow*. Maybe it was the title that stayed in readers' minds, but anyhow, through the years that have passed, I have been receiving letters from all parts of the English-speaking world, asking: 'When are you going to write another volume?' I wrote in the Prologue to *I Hate Tomorrow*: 'While I have been writing this book, the tramp of German soldiers has been growing louder; German armoured cars and tanks and airplanes rattle and roar across stricken Europe. . . .' Naturally, tragedy I foresaw, but I did not foresee that it would come down the streets in which I lived: the streets of Paris; so this book is a personal record of that story: the story of what really happened when France fell; or, if you will, a second volume in the story of my life.

When France fell in June, 1940, I fell with her. My life, lived in France for the previous thirty years, crumbled up; it had been a good life; an adventurous life, filled to the brim with the things a young Englishman did in those days, when he metaphorically threw his bowler hat over the windmill and went to live in Paris. I had never actually starved in a garret, but I had been exceedingly hungry in several near-garrets in Montmartre and on the Left Bank; although no Mimi ever pinned her shawl across the window of any abode of mine, I came to learn French by means of the traditional sleeping dictionary. Austen Chamberlain said one loved France as one loved a woman. How true; how very true. Although French-women have only possessed the right to vote for a comparatively short period, yet they have one way and another ruled the country for centuries, and the part they played in her downfall was not small. But just as one loves a woman for her faults, those of us who loved France love her still, despite the faults that brought her down.

I fell with France for the reason that my roots were deep down in her soil. In 1914 I had married an Alsatian woman, at a time when Alsace meant so much to France; mere sentimentality as I see it now, but glorious patriotism as I then believed it to be. Our daughter was born in Paris. I had struggled hard but successfully towards my goal. I had been a mail clerk, salesman, tutor, free-lance journalist; my hungry days spent in poverty had drawn me in closer and closer understanding with the French people. Then I joined the staff, a humble junior, of the Paris *Daily Mail*, and so finally came into my own a little later, as Paris correspondent of one of the great London daily newspapers. During those twenty years, lush years of splendour, I had been behind the scenes in all the French ministerial and financial crises. With the French people I had loved and hated and despaired and triumphed. I was perhaps no more than a recorder and commentator, a super in the glittering cavalcade, but I felt myself to be a part of it, and maybe for that very reason my work shone all the brighter. Best of all, I retained Paris as my base while I travelled the world, always coming back to the loveliest of cities, ready to fall in love with it all over again, but with eyes all the clearer for my absences, eyes able to penetrate deeply into the murky depths of the politico-financial scandals that lay below the surface of the effervescing French life.

Then came yet another facet of my French life. I grew tired of the hurly-burly of reporting; the period of objective reporting passed with the speeding up of transmission. Just as the typewriter has replaced the pen, so had the improved telephone service and the teleprinter replaced the typewriter; one no longer had time to think, to reflect on the interpretation of news. Then, as the storm clouds gathered, I withdrew from reporting their movement. I wanted to draw on my stored-up knowledge, gained from the pages of living history. I wanted to write, with due reflection primed with understanding. This I was doing, not unsuccessfully, when France fell.

With many others I offered my services here and there; to

the British authorities in Paris. I was sent to London; I was sent back to Paris. I offered my services to France, and the French were as frustrating as the British. Then I was offered a post with the British, but because I did not ask for enough money, I was rejected, and then contacted again just as the *débâcle* happened. For reasons I shall explain, I had to go into hiding. I emerged to try and leave France. I met with a series of almost incredible adventures, which led me into the birth of the Resistance movement inside France; a development that had, in the beginning at least, absolutely no connection with anything that was happening on the British side of the Channel. Then I was rounded up and sent into 'forced residence', where my work with the loosely-linked resistance continued, until with my life in great danger, and my daughter threatened with forced labour in Germany, I contacted secret agents, and stood not on the order of our going from France. For those reasons, briefly and baldly exposed for the moment, I believe that my life in France before and during the Fall, and for two years during the Occupation, allows me to write objectively of what I know and what I saw, and what in a humble way I did.

This is a book about a certain historic aspect of France, written by an Englishman who wishes the truth to prevail. Others have written about France from the outside looking in; I am going to try and reverse that process.

My book falls, I think, into three natural sequences; Book I: Why France Fell; Book II: When France Fell; Book III: After France Fell.

H.J.G.

BOOK ONE

Chapter I

IN MAY, 1937, the Great French Exhibition was late getting under way because of the 'stay-in' strikes. They were called at first 'sit-down' strikes; they were imported from Poland, where the miners sat down in the mines and refused to work until their claims were satisfied. France took to the idea whole-heartedly. Abroad, principally in Britain and America, the newspapers were saying they were Communist-inspired strikes. In the beginning that was not true; later the Communists exploited those 'stay-in' strikes. But, not when they began. Strange scenes there were; the staff of the Trois Quartiers, a smart department store on the Boulevard des Capucines, staged a so-called 'stay-in' strike; the staff gave parties and dances inside the store.

I was living in a flat on the Quai de Javel alongside the Seine; my flat faced the Pont Mirabeau and I looked across the river into the windows of aristocratic Auteuil. But the Quai de Javel was not aristocratic: anything but that. Down the road and all around there were factories; one of them staged a 'stay-in' strike. Evidently the strikers found strike pay insufficient, so they made sorties to collect funds. One day I heard a noise, and went out on to my study balcony that faced down towards the city. In the middle distance was the replica of the Statue of Liberty the French had presented to New York. Madame Liberty used to face up river, but when the Exhibition building began, they turned the statue round on its base so that it faced down river towards Le Havre, presumably to greet the tourists arriving from the U.S.A. That morning as I looked down the street, I saw the local strikers, men and women, marching gaily along and rattling wooden collecting-boxes. When they saw me standing on the balcony they raised their clenched fists in the Communist salute and shouted: 'Come down and join us, Comrade!'. But I had my jobs to which I had to attend; my books and magazine articles to write. Across the Rhine, Adolf Hitler had for three years been making headway, although at just this time only a part of France was frightened of him. The rich and the near-rich looked to Hitler to protect them against Communism. 'Better Hitler than Communism', they said. It was not long since that France had been Communist-conscious. But now, up and down the country, the Communists were exploiting strikes and hindering the work of the new Government of which the Communists, nominally at least, formed part. At the recent General Election the 'Popular Front' had triumphed. This political cartel consisted of the Socialists, the Radical-Socialists and the Communists. The Radical-Socialists, however, are neither Radical nor Socialist: they are left-wing Liberals; for decades they had been numerically the strongest party in the country. The Socialists hitherto had always been more Fabian-minded than Marx-controlled; the Communists were purely Moscow-controlled Frenchmen. When the time came to form a 'Popular Front' Government the Communists stepped aside. They would support the Government, they said, but they would not participate in it. In other words, power without responsibility.

Léon Blum, the Socialist leader, was an intellectual Socialist who had never had to work for his living. He was a member of a rich Alsatian Jewish family, and a delightful conversationalist; his books of theatrical criticism were charming. He was extremely surprised when he was made Premier. In fact, it took him six weeks to overcome his surprise and form a Government. During those weeks, many things happened. The opening date of the Exhibition which was to bring in dollars and pounds, and still more, re-establish the prestige of France, was getting later and later, and across the Rhine the tramp of the *feldgrau* men was growing louder and louder. At this moment, poor Monsieur Blum was being urged to nationalise all industries including railways and coal mines and to give the workers paid holidays. He made a sudden rush and plunged France into industrial chaos. What it had taken Britain a century to accomplish, Blum did in a matter of months. But among his Radical-Socialist colleagues there was growing dissension.

For years the party had been presided over by the perpetual Mayor of Lyons, the stout and hearty but now ageing Edouard Herriot. Monsieur Herriot had been Premier and had held other ranks in French government. Now one of his former pupils, Edouard Daladier, was elbowing his former master out of his way. Daladier the baker's son seemed destined for power, but he had been in office at the time of the Stavisky riots. It was he who ordered the troops to fire on the rioting crowds trying to cross the Concorde Bridge to attack the Chamber of Deputies. I was on the other side of the world, in China and Japan, at the time of the Stavisky riots, but I had known Daladier formerly. Naturally I did not see him again until after I returned to France, when I was startled to see a frightened look in those blue eyes of his, a look he has never lost; he wears it still: a mirror reflecting the memory of those February evenings when the rifle shots in the Place de la Concorde played the same part the bomb did that June Sunday afternoon in Sarajevo.

France was most unfortunate in those pre-war years, 1937 to 1939. The French men and women who admired Hitler so much because he 'kept Communists in their place' were equally appreciative of his treatment of the Jews. Ever since that Dreyfus affair, anti-Semitism had been latent in France; it needed so little to bring it to the surface. The advent of the Jew, Léon Blum, was all that was required. Separating the Jewish Socialist Blum from the Radical-Socialists was nothing but a narrow gap. That gap was so easily bridged by the French Freemasons. The French Freemasons are known colloquially in France as 'La Rue Cadet', which requires a little explanation.

French Freemasonry, unrecognised by the Grand Lodge of Great Britain, is known as the Lodge of the Orient. It has its headquarters in the Rue Cadet, which is the Parisian Hatton Garden. Its purposes are purely political. It is anti-clerical, and it is the spiritual home of the French free-thinkers. The vast majority of the Radical-Socialists are French Freemasons. So, for the purpose of Hitler's propaganda, you had a French Government composed of Jews and Freemasons. This was seized on by the French clericals, orthodox Roman Catholics, and the rich who did not ordinarily give the Church their support. But they united in paying tribute to Hitler because it suited their pockets, or so they thought at the time. Never was France worse served than she was as from the victory of the 'Popular Front'. God knows that the workers were badly paid and entitled to higher wages and better conditions. But the weakness of the Socialists and the Radical-Socialists lay in their foolish alliance with the Communists. The honeymoon did not last long, but long enough to conceive a child that was to take France to the precipice and push her over.

At last the Great Exhibition opened, and it was wonderful. Paris is the ideal city for shows of this kind, but the centre-piece, as it were, was sinister indeed. Facing each other like giants biting their thumbs at one another were the Russian and German pavilions. From my study windows I could see them, dominating everything; ugly buildings housing ugly things, and in startling contrast to the beautiful things France wanted to show the world. It was pathetic. It recalled to my mind a cartoon that had appeared in *L'Humanité* not long after the first world war. Marianne, a somewhat decrepit old lady with a raddled face, was seated in an armchair. Standing round her were her wartime allies, Britain, America, Belgium and Italy. Marianne was saying: '*Chantez encore une fois avec moi, que je suis jeune et belle.*' Now, some seventeen years later,

16

France was still trying to persuade the world that she was young and beautiful. And we others with our wishful thinking did so try and persuade both France and ourselves.

But the moles were at work digging tunnels beneath the fair enough looking surface. There was for example a weekly paper called *Gringoire*, owned and edited by the son-in-law of the Paris Prefect of Police, Jean Chiappe. Chiappe, a Fascist, had been dismissed for the part he played—or did not play—in the Stavisky riots. *Gringoire* was an anti-semitic, anti-British organ, written with great wit but with pens dipped in vitriol. There was another witty weekly, *Le Canard Enchainé*, with no political bias. When Chiappe was dismissed there was controversy as to what he had said when he had telephoned the Minister of the Interior. The Minister claimed Chiappe had said: '*Je serais sur la rue ce soir*', which the Minister regarded as a threat, meaning: 'I shall be on the street tonight'; in other words, leading an attack as the Stavisky rioters did. Chiappe claimed he had said: '*Je serais dans la rue ce soir*', 'I shall be in the street tonight', which a Frenchman says when he has been sacked, like the English 'thrown in the street'.

The *Canard Enchainé* had its own version. What Chiappe really said was: '*Je serais chez Larue ce soir.*' Larue, at the right-hand corner of the Rue Royale, opposite the Madeleine, was still at that time the expensive restaurant frequented by politicians. Many a Government has been overthrown at a small select party held in one of Larue's private rooms.

A bad situation was made worse by deceptive newspaper reporting abroad; events of vital import in both France and Germany were badly recorded in the British Press, mainly because three correspondents, two in Berlin and one in Paris, seemingly allowed their personal feelings to colour their reports. In Berlin the Nazis simplified matters by expelling British correspondents whose factual reports they did not approve. Berlin correspondents of two British newspapers were expelled, but in the case of the Berlin-born correspondent of a London newspaper with an enormous circulation, the Nazis gave him every facility to boom and boost Hitler in Britain. In Paris a British subject of foreign ancestry was the correspondent of a newspaper with a large circulation. The proprietor of this newspaper was not only a fervent admirer of Hitler, but he also underwrote the hire of Olympia for a rally of Sir Oswald Mosley's British Union of Fascists. The Berlin correspondent of the same newspaper at this time was also of Fascist mentality. He was a fervent Roman Catholic, as was his opposite number in Paris. These men distorted their reports from their respective capitals. Thus millions of British readers were obtaining untruthful reports from Berlin and Paris at a time when Britain should have been made aware of the truth in all its shocking nudity.

The French Press was even worse served. All through the history of the Third Republic the French Press had received bribes from the Government of the day; that was an accepted tradition. When Léon Blum came to power, he announced that he was going to abolish the secret fund that had been at the disposal of the French Governments. I believe that he did as he said, but in the event it proved to be a useless gesture, because the secret payments continued in another guise. For instance, Jules Sauerwein of the *Matin* was in the pay of Pierre Laval. Sauerwein was dismissed from the *Matin* because he did not share with that newspaper the private monies he was receiving, not only from Laval, but also from the Polish and Japanese Governments. That did not worry Sauerwein at all, because he merely went from the *Matin* to a Parisian evening newspaper, where he continued to be in the pay of Pierre Laval. His leaving the *Matin* led to a most interesting telephonic conversation. Laval had given Sauerwein certain instructions about the writing of an article. Either Sauerwein misunderstood his instructions, or he wilfully disobeyed them. When the article appeared, Laval was very annoyed, so he telephoned the editor of the *Matin*, who as a matter of fact is now serving a prison sentence because he was found guilty of being a traitor, and told him that Sauerwein had not obeyed his order. The editor

18

replied that, after all, Sauerwein was employed by the *Matin* and not by Monsieur Laval. Laval snapped back: 'But I pay him more than you do, so he must do as I tell him.' That led up to the dismissal. I myself heard the editor say in my presence: 'I don't blame Jules so much for accepting money, but after all, he might have split fifty-fifty with us.'

As the months passed I was to become in closer contact with many other Frenchmen who were the gravediggers of their country. It was an amazing thing, amazing to me at any rate, this deterioration of the French; somebody, I think it was myself, had once written that a Frenchman would die for his country although he would not pay for it. But now in this twilight period, Jean Français was a defeatist; his cynicism was almost unbelievable. Yet there are many people who still believe the French in 1937 and onwards to September 1939 thought that war was inevitable. This was emphatically not so. The truth, as I am trying to tell it, proves that too many people in France thought only of themselves; how to profit from the war should it come; how to profit from such circumstances that would arise if war was avoided.

In June 1938, it was decided to overthrow the Blum Government. There was a luncheon party in a private room at the restaurant Larue. The guest of honour was Senator Joseph Caillaux, a politician whose political life had been cut short by Georges Clemenceau. But now the old 'Tiger' was dead. Caillaux was very much alive. Caillaux's hosts were some leading bankers. During lunch they planned a scheme to discredit the Blum Government. A few days after the lunch, Pierre Baudouin, a close friend of Laval, and Charles Rist, Governor of the Bank of France, resigned from the Exchange Control Committee; the Bank of France's re-discount rate leaped from four to six per cent. Capital began to flee from France. Premier Blum asked the Chamber for decree powers, as Caillaux had done some years earlier, when Herriot had opposed and defeated him, but Blum obtained his powers. Now he had to go to the Senate, where Caillaux waited for him.

Caillaux made a sneering attack on Blum; Laval supported him, and the Blum Government toppled over.

Caillaux was now the power behind the French scene. With Senator de Monzie, a politician who profited financially through politico-financial activities, he manoeuvred to make Edouard Daladier Premier, by persuading sufficient Deputies and Senators that by separating Blum from Daladier that would end the possibility of another 'Popular Front' Government. Caillaux, however, extracted promises from Daladier; he was not to support Czechoslovakia, and he was to come to terms with Hitler. Daladier hesitated, but he finally accepted.

Later, when Daladier became Premier of France, several British newspapers referred to him as 'The Bull' and said that that was his nickname in France. I had never heard it. The truth about Edouard Daladier, who was Prime Minister at a very vital period in French history, can be told very simply.

He was a widower, with an only son. He lived in a fine house in the rue de la Faisanderie, off the Avenue du Bois de Boulogne. For about three years, since the time of the Stavisky riots, he had become much addicted to the more potent of French *aperitifs*. French diplomatic correspondents never sought to see him after the first part of the morning. He stopped working regularly about 11.30, then he began drinking *pastis*. Daladier at the crucial time of his political career was entirely under the influence of the Marquise Marie Louise de Crussols d'Uzès. She was a member of a wealthy family that had made a fortune out of the sardine canning industry at Douarnenez. She married the grandson of the famous Dowager Duchess of Uzès, whom I used to see regularly at Chantilly at the meets of the Duc de Grammont's stag hunts. She would sit frisky hunters, a large cigar stuck in her mouth. Her grandson's wife's political *salon* in Paris was frequented by diplomats, financiers and parliamentarians. Parisian journalistic circles knew that Daladier never took a decision without reference to Madame la Marquise.

Daladier, I would say, was a weak man in politics and in a way the victim of circumstances, and among those 'circumstances' I would name Gaston Doumergue, a minor politician who was destined to become President of France. He was known to fame as the man who married his mistress a week before his term of office expired. When asked why he did that, he explained cynically: 'So that for one week at least she could call herself *Madame la Présidente.*' Doumergue was known up and down France affectionately as 'Gastounet'; people said: 'He has such a nice face.' He had indeed, but to my mind he was a very sinister person. He was nothing more nor less than a creature of the Fascist private army known as the *Croix de Feu.*

Doumergue was called back from retirement after his term as President of the Republic came to an end, in order to form a Government after the Stavisky riots in 1934. He was then seventy-two years of age. Doumergue said he was going to revise the Constitution, but two hours before he was due to form his Ministry, street-fighting broke out in Paris, and three days later there was a general strike throughout France. Doumergue and his backers became frightened, because this was the first joint demonstration of Socialists and Communists since 1922, when the two parties had split. But Doumergue formed his Government of twenty-four; among those two dozen there was much dissent. There was André Tardieu, for instance, who wanted France to become a corporate state, just like Italy. Then there was Pierre Laval, who wanted France to go Fascist and to co-operate with Fascist Germany and Fascist Italy. But Louis Barthou, who was seventy-two years of age, had quite another point of view. He was Minister of Foreign Affairs, and he was eager to find new allies for France to keep Germany at bay. But behind his back Pierre Laval was negotiating with Hitler. There are good grounds for believing that Laval knew of the plot to assassinate Barthou at Marseilles. After the assassination, Pierre Laval replaced him in the French Foreign Office.

Another strange person who was in the Cabinet was Pierre Etienne Flandin, a man who spoke fluent English and at that time was very familiar with what was known as the 'Cliveden Set'. Flandin was on very intimate terms with a prominent British newspaper proprietor; their wives were very friendly. Flandin used to go frequently to England and stay with his friends. Before entering politics, he was a lawyer and became involved in the very notorious and unpleasant Aero-Poste scandal, but that did not prevent him duly becoming Premier. I believe that he helped to dig France's grave by encouraging Hitler, to whom he sent a telegram of congratulation when Hitler re-entered the Rhineland.

André Tardieu was known in journalistic circles in Paris as 'The Shark'; in fact his head bore a very striking resemblance to a shark. Tardieu was a brilliant journalist and a protégé of Clemenceau, who brought him into politics, but Tardieu gave over his life to the society of women. Even when he attended a political conference in London, and stayed at the Carlton Hotel, he was accompanied by a then very prominent actress of the Comédie Française. As Tardieu grew more and more weary, he became more and more Fascist-minded. Not only did he wish to turn France into a corporate state, but when he was at the Ministry of the Interior, he subsidised Colonel de la Rocque, who was the head of the *Croix de Feu*.

Another man who was what in Britain would have been termed 'a queer fish' was Georges Bonnet. Bonnet was the son of a French county court judge; he became a lawyer, and was a sergeant in the first world war. He obtained a commission from the ranks, a very unusual occurrence in the French army. Bonnet attracted much attention in 1919, because of the good work he did when the army was demobilised. This brought him into contact with the leading financiers and industrialists. In 1942 Bonnet became a Deputy and he was the parliamentary lobbyist for a group of industrialists. He naturally drifted towards the Radical-Socialist party and consolidated his standing within the party by marrying Odette Pelletin, who was the niece of a former chairman of the party. She was an extremely ambitious woman, who worked hard to further her husband's interests. Her name became closely linked with that of von Ribbentrop.

Bonnet's work in the Chamber attracted the attention of one of the leading Paris bankers, and soon Bonnet was working under cover for the bank. In 1933 Bonnet was Minister of Finance, and two years later Minister of Commerce, and two years after that he went to Washington as Ambassador, and then returned to France and became Minister of Finance once again. Then later he was Minister for Foreign Affairs, and then after that he was Minister of Justice. He was never out of the picture, and he undoubtedly did more to bring about the downfall of France than any other prominent politician of the day.

Georges Bonnet's rise to power coincided with the Nazi's seizure of power. In 1938, Bonnet, who was then in the Foreign Office, began a widespread campaign not only to corrupt, or perhaps it would be better to say more corrupt the French Press, but he also began to try and corrupt correspondents of the foreign Press. He did not have much success with the foreigners, but in one particular instance he was very successful. Every month Bonnet used to send out envelopes containing banknotes to some of his hand-picked journalist friends. He tried very hard to get the Paris correspondent of *The Times* expelled from France, and I understand he requested the late Sir Charles Mendl, the then Press Attaché of the British Embassy, to have me expelled. Two journalists, one British and the other a Scot, came under Bonnet's spell. The British journalist was the late Sisley Huddleston, a former Paris correspondent of *The Times* and of the *Christian Science Monitor*. The other man, the late Percy Phillip, was not bought with money, but with good dinners, flattery, and the promise of social advancement.

I was thinking on those things when one morning in 1938 I was standing on my balcony and idly looking down on the Seine. I noticed that French soldiers were being stationed at

23

about every six feet or so along the electric railway that paralleled the river. Then I remembered that von Ribbentrop was due that day in Paris to sign a treaty with his opposite number Georges Bonnet.

The man who brought about this meeting was Count Fernand de Brinon, who later introduced Otto Abetz to Georges Bonnet. Now let me introduce the Count de Brinon.

When Hitler was about to march into Vienna, a British newspaper group asked me to fly there to report the event. There was an acquaintance and former neighbour of mine on the plane: Count Fernand de Brinon, a man who was a little later to acquire considerable notoriety before he met death at the hands of a firing squad composed of his compatriots. The Count and I both lived for a number of years in a block of flats called the Square des Aigles, at Chantilly. He married a French Jewess, a Mademoiselle Bernheim, a member of the family that owns the famous Parisian art gallery. Fernand de Brinon was a writer on the staff of the Paris daily financial newspaper L'Information. We had been in London together to report the Ramsay MacDonald sponsored Naval Conference, but what really interested me about the man was his gambling proclivity. Chantilly is the great French racing centre; de Brinon backed horses heavily and, according to rumour, unsuccessfully. He was always in debt, but latterly his fortunes seemed to have prospered. And now he was sitting across the aisle from my seat on the Vienna-bound plane. He did not talk much, but we found ourselves in the same hotel, the Grand, so what could be more natural than that we should step out together to view the scene being set for Hitler's arrival?

I called de Brinon's attention to the absence of older people from the milling crowds in the Vienna streets, and the evident enthusiasm of the younger people. To which my companion replied: 'Ah, yes, my dear colleague, we must stress this in our reports; how enthusiastic are the Austrians for the coming of Hitler.' I was most embarrassed. I asked de Brinon for whom he was reporting; was it L'Information? He made an evasive reply, so it was not until my return to Paris that I obtained my answer.

Fernand de Brinon had been contacted by the Nazis soon after Hitler became Chancellor, on January 30th, 1933. It is usual for France to be without a Government whenever something serious happens, and this particular date was no exception. Through the good offices of Daladier's woman friend, the Marquise de Crussols d'Uzès, de Brinon entered into direct contact with Edouard Daladier. Later de Brinon asked Daladier to write a letter for him to take to Berlin; it was a request for an interview with Hitler. In November, 1933, de Brinon obtained his interview; Daladier asked the *Matin* to publish it, and it did. The interview boosted Hitler, who said, notably: 'Those who say I want war insult me; I am not that sort of man. War? It would settle nothing. . . . It would mark the end of our races, which are the élite of the world.' This interview had a great effect on France. It became known that Daladier had sponsored it, so it helped Daladier in his political career. A few months later, as I have written, he had a setback on account of the Stavisky riots, but four years later he was at the head of the Government that succeeded the 'Popular Front'.

In March, 1938, Hitler annexed Austria, and here again was Fernand de Brinon, with journalistic credentials, but now really a personal representative of the French Premier. After that his rise was rapid.

It was now a Wednesday morning in 1938, and the French soldiery were guarding the railway track to the Gare des Invalides. Trains from Berlin to Paris were scheduled to arrive at the Gare du Nord. Why then was Ribbentrop's train going somewhere else? I was to learn why a little later that morning. As I said, it was a Wednesday, and I was due to lunch *chez* Madame Geneviève Tabouis. One always heard interesting things at lunch *chez* Madame Tabouis.

Chapter II

To UNDERSTAND Madame Tabouis one must understand her background. *L'Oeuvre* was a wittily written Paris daily newspaper, what is called *un journal d'opinion* rather than *un journal d'information:* editorial opinions rather than news. It was well known and often quoted for its foreign *news* as well as its views, because the newspaper specialised in foreign affairs, but its editor-proprietor Jean Piot was one of the most venal of the Parisian venal journalists of the period immediately leading to the downfall of France.

L'Oeuvre's editorial offices were in the rue d'Antin, just around the corner from Harry's New York Bar in the rue Daunau. Piot was a tall, heavily-built middle-aged man, a hearty drinker who used to enter the New York Bar about nine every night shouting aloud to Charley the barman: 'Give me a Scotch whisky in order that I shall have some very French ideas!' But how really French those ideas were it would be difficult to say. Piot would sit in the bar until he was befuddled; then he would march in a drunken dignified manner back to his editorial office and proceed to produce a brilliant newspaper.

Camille Lemercier was the first foreign affairs columnist on *L'Oeuvre*, and very good and sound he was; he left in order to earn more money in the Paris office of an American newspaper. But he died, quite young. He was succeeded by Madame Geneviève Tabouis.

She first entered the political scene at Geneva in the heyday of the League of Nations; regularly she attended the meetings of the Council and the Assembly. Although very *petite* and frail-looking (she had had a kidney removed, like the German Chancellor of the time), she invariably attracted attention. 'Who's that?' people asked one another as she passed by. She always wore black and she was always very chic; her almost white hair was always most beautifully dressed. She seldom smiled. She was, I suppose, the first woman journalist to specialise in foreign affairs. Gradually she became a sort of oracle; she was often completely wrong on points of factual importance, and her forecasts were frequently right off the target, but her readers forgot her errors and remembered only her exclusive statements that were completely accurate. When French Foreign Ministers visited foreign capitals, she went along too. She gave her readers the impression that she was right under the table around which the Ministers conferred. Those who have been in contact with French politicians know that they above any other nationals are the most indiscreet; often on purpose, let me add. For decades they have practised the art of official leakage, an art the Americans are now learning. But although Madame Tabouis was on friendly terms with many members of successive French cabinets, they were not her main sources of information.

Madame Tabouis was related by birth to a number of prominent French Foreign Office officials; the Cambons, who for two generations at least had peopled the French Embassies in many countries, were her uncles and cousins. Through them she had contacts with other French diplomats. At night, before she began to write her daily column on foreign affairs, she would turn herself into a one-woman international telephone exchange; she would ring up London, Rome, Berne, Berlin, anywhere, and talk to the French Embassies there. The sum total of her talks would appear in *L'Oeuvre* the following morning, but it was too much to expect that her contacts provided her with all the exciting things she told her readers; whence did those things come? Madame Tabouis was a woman of great sincerity, but what she thought to be so, was so; she had the ability to persuade herself that things happened the way she thought they should happen. More and more frequently she was quoted in the foreign press. Then one day a London publisher asked me if I could persuade her to write a book about foreign affairs. I discussed the matter with her; she was most willing. We discussed a title; facetiously I suggested: 'Perfidious Albion'. To my surprise, she thought that a splendid idea, so I insisted that there should be an exclamation mark after Albion.

Madame Tabouis could not speak or write English; she asked me if I would translate her book. I agreed, and in due course I received some sheets torn from her daughter's school exercise-book, and covered in her handwriting. It was the first chapter of her book.

The first chapter referred to the premiership of Joseph Chamberlain (who of course was never of higher rank than that of Colonial Secretary) and she made a mistake of a hundred years in the date of the Siege of Calais. I returned the chapter, pointed out the mistakes, and said that I found to my regret that I was too busy to undertake the translation. The book was published, and I am sorry to say that it was a dismal failure. But that did not disturb our friendship.

I have chosen to write the story of Madame Tabouis because in her way she was one of the innocent contributing causes to the fall of France. Other women ran their salons, but Geneviève ran luncheon parties every Wednesday, when her guests were almost always people in the forefront of French political life to which could be added people who, in the past, had played prominent parts in world affairs, and who now spoke from the shadows, but they uttered remarks that sometimes brilliantly illuminated the historical past.

Madame Tabouis had a large apartment at 24 Place Malsherbes. Monsieur Tabouis, younger than Madame I would say, I met but once; he was vaguely connected with the French film industry. They had a son in the army, and an invalid daughter in Switzerland. On the Wednesday to which I made reference, I sat next to Monsieur Roger Langeron, who had succeeded Jean Chiappe as Paris Prefect of Police. I told the Prefect what I had just seen from my study window, the soldiers guarding the railway track for von Ribbentrop to ride into a quiet out-of-the-way railway station. I asked if there was any reason; was there any danger of him being assassinated? Monsieur Langeron answered without hesitation that he would be very glad when von Ribbentrop went back to Berlin, because Nazi *agents provocateurs* might stage a fake assassination in order to start trouble in Paris. That brief conversation I mention as being illustrative of the atmosphere in which we in Paris lived in those days of 1938 as the world edged nearer and nearer to war.

That Wednesday I met General Robert of the French Army, and asked him his opinion of the Russian Army. Straight away he said that the Russians would fight magnificently so long as they fought on Russian soil, defending their country, but they would be of no use at all if they had to fight on foreign soil. Another illustration of things said by people who were supposed to know.

Kaleidoscopic pictures of personalities attending those Wednesday lunches come to mind. There was Georges Mandel, at long last arrived at the place of his heart's desire, the Ministry of the Interior, the key post in the Cabinet; previously he had been Minister of Colonies, and prior to that Minister of the Post and Telegraph. Mandel was a man of mystery, a French Jew, whose real name was Rothschild. He was supposed to be a natural son of Georges Clemenceau, to whom he bore a certain physical resemblance. Mandel always wore what appeared to me to be a sort of uniform: a blue suit and a very high white stiff collar. He had a pale face, he wore his hair parted in the middle, and he had a cold fishy stare.

Mandel was very much a protégé of Clemenceau. We first hear of him during the 1914-18 war, when Clemenceau launched a newspaper called *L'Homme Libre*. Mandel was his editorial factotum. When Poincaré ended his feud with Clemenceau and made him Premier, Clemenceau made Mandel his political secretary. Then Mandel entered politics on his own account and sat in the Chamber of Deputies for a Bordeaux constituency. He came to a Tabouis lunch one day with a fair-haired beauteous lady, to whom we were not introduced, but of whom it was said that she was a member of the Comédie Française company. Was Georges Mandel running true to tradition? From time immemorial it was customary for a French Cabinet Minister to choose a mistress from the cast of that famous theatre at the foot of the Avenue de l'Opéra; elderly Senators chose theirs from the theatre at the top end of the Avenue, the Opéra itself, and from among the members of the *corps de ballet*. Mandel at this particular lunch talked at length about colonies, and Hitler's alleged desire to obtain some. Fixing me with his cold fishy stare, Mandel said very clearly that if it came to the question of countries surrendering the colonies they held, Britain would have to surrender some of hers. I felt most uncomfortable. Mandel reappears later in this narrative.

Raoul Paternôtre was another guest at one party. He had recently become Under-Secretary for Air. He was young middle-aged, more than six feet tall, and much addicted to drugs and women. He was very handsome, and one of the richest men in France. His father had once been French Ambassador in Washington, and had married an American millionairess, who adored their only son, and had given him a million francs on his fourteenth birthday. He had lived on that standard ever since. Paternôtre was a Paris neighbour of Edouard Daladier.

Not at this lunch was Paternôtre's 'grey eminence', whom I came to know very well; he was a Jewish Luxemburger whose name is Pierre Wolf. Wolf, when he first met Paternôtre, was a ship's barber aboard the *Isle de France*. Wolf twice saved his patron's fortune; he has the Midas touch. At that moment, in 1939, Paternôtre owned separately or in partnership with Wolf, *L'Auto*, a powerful Paris daily newspaper that took a 'rake-off' from every major sporting event in France; *Marianne*, a weekly publication; also morning and evening newspapers in Lyons; the Hotel Royal in Nice, and La Poularde, one of the best-known restaurants in the city (Madame Wolf ran a kosher restaurant there).

They likewise owned *Le Petit Niçois*, one of the most important newspapers on the French Riviera. At the time I met Paternôtre, at lunch, he and Pierre Wolf were about to go to the south of France to buy up some land 'in case of war'.

Yet another guest on another day was Albert Sarrault, whose contribution to the downfall of France was not altogether slight. He and his brother owned the Radical *Dépêche de Toulouse*, incidentally at that time one of the best of the French provincial newspapers. Albert Sarrault was one of the pillars of the Radical-Socialist party. He had been Prime Minister, and held office very often. He had been Ambassador at Constantinople, Governor of Indo-China, and during the Dreyfus affair, he had fought a duel in Paris, and still carried the scar. His chief interests, however, were food and women; he had the reputation of being a great epicure and a great lover. He was indeed still a power behind the French political scene, and was soon back in office during these critical days, but now this ageing Casanova sat at Geneviève Tabouis' table, exchanging conversation with Signor Nitti, the former Prime Minister of Italy, the last of the surviving signatories of the Treaty of Versailles; Lloyd George, Clemenceau and President Wilson were dead; those others who had also signed for France, Stéphen, Pichon and David Klotz, had died in mental asylums, the latter after serving a prison sentence for uttering false cheques. But Signor Nitti, a refugee from Mussolini, lived in exile in straitened circumstances in Paris.

Nitti said that day that Hitler must fight but Mussolini should not. In view of the behind-the-scenes part Nitti tried to play in preparing the surrender of Italy in 1945, this opinion expressed four months before Italy entered the war is not without interest, I think. After saying what I have quoted about Mussolini, Signor Nitti then told us that he had in his possession a letter from King George V thanking him for opposing the plan to hang the Kaiser. He said that President Wilson was neutral, but that Lloyd George and Clemenceau really wanted to hang the Kaiser. At the time, I regarded Signor Nitti's story with some doubt, but since then Lord Beaverbrook has published his book, *Men and Power*, and produced documentary evidence that Signor Nitti was right. So King George did not want his cousin hanged, a very human sentiment. But I have had ample proof of how royalty lives in a close corporation. When King Constantine of Greece was in exile in a hotel in Lucerne, he showed me a letter from King George V wishing him well, and expressing the hope that he would regain his throne. In Madrid, King Alfonso asked me if it was true that King George V had been hooted in Manchester in 1917. It was true, but I did not know it at the time. However, King Alfonso requested me to ask the British Ambassador, and let him know privately. It is clear that kings must hang together, otherwise. . . .

But to return *chez* Tabouis; what did our hostess have to say at her own table? Poor Geneviève Tabouis: she served exquisite food that drew compliments from gourmets such as Albert Sarrault, but on account of her missing kidney, she sat there nibbling a salad. She acted like a Greek chorus, commenting on the remarks that criss-crossed her table. She was usually querulous and a little bitter about Britain. Sir Eric Phipps was British Ambassador at this time. She said that he was on too friendly terms with the Foreign Minister, Georges Bonnet. 'He can refuse him nothing', she said. She repeated an alleged *boutade* of Phipps: 'Speaking of a French Minister of Finance is like talking about a Swiss Minister of Marine'. Then she was very disparaging about the British Army: 'Only *two* armoured divisions', she moaned. Leslie Hore-Belisha was then Secretary for War, and he was attending the French military manoeuvres. Madame Tabouis said he was very patronising to the French Army, metaphorically patted it on the back, and said: '*Bravo, ma petite armée française!*'

In these thumbnail sketches, so to speak, of the people who played their innocent or guilty parts in the prelude to the fall of France, it is not possible to exclude some whose acts were so monstrous that their portraits require a broader canvas. Such a person was Pierre Laval. Much has been written about this man, who met a traitor's death at the hands of a French firing squad. This, on the other hand, is a personal picture. I met Laval for the first time in a *bistro* in St Denis, the working-class suburb on the north side of Paris. He came in wearing a cap and a white woollen muffler round his neck. When he loosened the muffler, I noticed he was wearing a white evening dress bow; what the orchid and the monocle were to Joseph Chamberlain, the white dress bow was to Pierre Laval; as he climbed to power he clung to the white bow. His enemies used to say: 'That is the only clean thing about him.'

I was in the *bistro* with a French political journalist, the late Léon Bassée of the Agence Havas. It was the time when the Communists were beginning to make their influence felt, and their headquarters were in St Denis. So nervous was the Government of the moment, that it brought a regiment of Moroccan cavalry, the Spahis, from North Africa, and stationed it at Senlis, a little further north than St Denis.

Laval's visits to the *bistros* at St Denis were frequent, so I learned from Bassée. Laval was a lawyer and a member of the Radical-Socialist party; he was very left-wing at the time; he began his political career as a Socialist, a protégé of Aristide Briand, also a lawyer, who entered Parliament as a Socialist; he then became a Liberal, or, in French, a Radical-Socialist. Laval, however, moved further and further to the Right; the higher he went, the more reactionary he became, but when I met him for the first time, he was 'one of the people'; not only did he dress the part, but his clients were workmen. Pierre Laval had an olive-green complexion; his looks were repulsive. Laval knew Bassée, and obviously knew of his importance. One could not help noticing that; he talked to him with respect.

Soon after this meeting Laval's rise was phenomenal. He ceased to be a poor man's lawyer; he was now a 'big shot', a highly paid legal adviser to some of the biggest French industrial concerns. He was popular with the public; he was a living success story, but just one little thing proved his undoing.

He had one child, a daughter named Josephine, who married

a son of Count de Chambrun, a descendant of the famous de Chambrun who was Lafayette's right hand. Now it is the dream of all the French *petit bourgeois* to give their daughters a *dot*, a dowry, no matter how small. In France it is a social dishonour, like not being able to pay your rent, if you do not give your daughter a dowry when she marries. But times had been hard in France; *les petit rentiers*, the people with fixed incomes, had had, since about 1920 when the franc began to crumple up, a hard struggle; and *dots* were very small indeed. Then came the Laval-de Chambrun marriage; quite a social climb for the daughter of the son of a pig farmer in the Auvergne. And then came the big news: Pierre Laval had given his daughter no less than about £100,000 as a dowry! That certainly caused a stir. From whence had Laval obtained the money? Nobody knew until many years later. The Auvergnards are reputed to be the meanest and most miserly of Frenchmen. And that caused all the more comment. People were suspicious now of Laval. They did not know at the time that he dabbled in every puddle of muddy financial water; through nominees he had interests in French licensed 'houses of joy'; his agents peddled shares in non-existent gold mines— always bait for the French peasantry. His connections with shady financial houses operating on the Paris Bourse were not known about until later. Nevertheless, his march to power kept in step with his approach to great financial heights.

When Briand was a tired old man, Laval clung close to him, and with his influence followed Louis Barthou into the Quai d'Orsay, as I have already related. For fifteen disastrous months Laval guided the foreign relations of the Third Republic. He was Foreign Minister under Flandin's Government, which lasted seven months. Flandin fell and was succeeded by Laval's friend Fernand Bouisson's Government, which lived for one day. There was the usual political crisis.

The Anglo-American Press of Paris was holding its annual dinner, always a glittering occasion. George Slocombe, who was its President in that particular year, was arranging the seating arrangements. He telephoned to me to say: 'I'm putting you next to Pierre Laval; is that all right?'

'No', I said, 'please don't; I can't stand the man.'

'All right, then', said Slocombe, 'I'll put you next to Tyrrell.' At that time Lord Tyrrell was British Ambassador in Paris.

We dined—late. The political crisis was still in being, when we sat down to our late dinner. I noticed there was an empty seat at our table. I looked at the place-card: it said Monsieur Pierre Laval.

Cabaret acts were taking place on the floor around which were our tables. The spotlight was on a dancer who was just making her exit. There was applause, then loud exclamations of surprise. I looked up. Now under the spotlight was Pierre Laval, wearing his white tie, also immaculate 'tails'. He was shown to his place. He smiled and bowed, greeted the Ambassador and sat down. He looked round and announced that he had just agreed to form a Government.

He was Prime Minister of France.

Chapter III

MEN LIKE PIERRE LAVAL played their part in the fall of France, but their misdeeds carried on after surrender; therefore they became part and parcel of the narrative and people in the procession I am seeking to describe. Marshal Pétain on the other hand had once completely vanished from the French scene; he was a forgotten man; his Verdun halo had faded; it was difficult to believe that this mediocre old soldier, for mediocre he was, should emerge from the shadows to become a world figure at an age when most old soldiers doze in the sun and dream of past battles lost and won. Those who know the real Pétain story often wonder how in the world he did become known as a great military hero. The Army hated him.

Henri Philippe Pétain was educated at Saint Cyr, the French Sandhurst. In 1914 he was fifty-nine years of age and only a colonel, but he commanded an infantry brigade. In the Army files his dossier was marked: 'Not to be permitted to be promoted higher than brigadier-general.' But in 1917 he was Commander-in-Chief of the French Army, chiefly because wartime political intrigues and military failures had unseated those superior in rank. During the earlier part of the war the Army hated his name because it was alleged that his inefficient military tactics had caused the French heavy losses, but at the Battle of Verdun he was supposed to have said: 'They shall not pass.' This occurred when the tide of battle turned in favour of the French, so the civilians adored him. In 1917, however, there occurred a mutiny in the French Army, news of which was naturally suppressed. The mutiny occurred on the battle-field of what was known as the *Chemin des Dames*; from this Ladies' Way, the mutineers decided to march on Paris, and imprison the Government and end the war. Only a battalion of the Foreign Legion barred the road to Paris. Pétain broke the mutiny by having every tenth man of the mutineers shot.

After the war he retired, but in 1935 he was brought out of retirement to subdue the Riff revolt in North Africa. One of his staff officers at this time was Colonel de la Rocque, who ten years later was leader of the Fascist *Croix de Feu*. Pétain in its formative years became its hero.

When Gaston Doumergue formed his Government after the Stavisky riots, Pétain was his Minister of War. Between 1925 and 1934 he was a neighbour of mine: a very small man, I used to see him battling against the elements, holding an open umbrella in front of him as he fought his way against the wind and rain on his way to Sunday morning Mass. We both lived at Chantilly; Pétain was the Curator of the Castle.

After Raymond Poincaré retired from political life he wrote his autobiography in ten volumes; in the last volume he wrote what he really thought and knew about Pétain. Poincaré said that in the first war Pétain was a defeatist who wished to surrender to Germany. As soon as Pétain became Leader of France, after her downfall, one of the first of the old Marshal's acts was to order the confiscation of the tenth volume of Poincaré's memoirs, a book that carried a report of his shame. The book was withdrawn from all public libraries in unoccupied France. I was in that part of France at the time, and I personally vouch for the authenticity of the story.

Pétain was only a short time at the Ministry of War, but long enough to give him a taste of what power can mean to an old man. Like many of the French Roman Catholics, he was a Royalist, and his fear of Communism caused him to take the same road so many other highly placed Frenchmen took: the road towards appeasing Hitler.

When Pétain was at the Ecole Militaire, Francisco Franco was one of his admiring pupils; when Franco won the Spanish Civil War, Pétain was sent to Madrid as Ambassador. It was there he met Hitler's ambassador, the late Eberhard von Stohrer; the two became fast friends. Pétain was still at his post when the 1939 war broke out, and a month later he was photographed warmly shaking hands with von Stohrer as the two men left a Roman Catholic service at the Monastery Real de los Huelgas. This picture shocked France, but the people of France would have been shocked still more had they known that Pétain was betraying them. Throughout the war, from September, 1939, until the surrender in June, 1940, Pétain remained in contact with the Nazi ambassador.

General Maxim Weygand was another curious personage in the procession I am describing, a cavalcade of people, civilians and military, jogging along towards the crucifixion of France on the Calvary of Vichy.

Weygand was always a man of mystery; his antecedents are even at this date unknown. He is understood to have been the son of a Belgian industrialist and a Polish woman. He was certainly the only man ever to become a French general without having passed through the Ecole Militaire. He had a good record in the first war, but was unknown to the French people until he was put in charge of an army that relieved Warsaw when it was being besieged by the Russian Bolsheviks. Clemenceau distrusted him. He dismissed him from conversation with one of his sarcastic wisecracks: 'Weygand? He's up to his neck in priests!' True, like Pétain, Weygand was a fervent Roman Catholic and became closely associated with various Fascist groups, not only the *Croix de Feu* but also the notorious 'Hooded Men', reports of whose alleged activities were greatly exaggerated in the British and American Press. But General Weygand was the accredited adviser to the various French Governments in the days when war was coming ever nearer. Weygand did not believe in the military might of the Germans, so he said; he believed that even as late as 1939, when he said it would take Germany at least another ten years to develop a military machine compatible with the one the Kaiser put into the field; he believed that Hitler's Germany lacked trained officers and trained reserves. But most of all Weygand believed in the power and the strength of the Maginot Line, and because General Maxim Weygand believed in those simple and touching faiths, the whole of France believed in them too, and the people thought themselves impregnable behind the Maginot Line, thought out by Maginot, a loose-living cripple of the first world war, who spent most of his evenings holding court in the genial atmosphere of the bar *chez* Maxim.

If Weygand was wrong about the Germans, he, like General Ironside, was right about the strength of the Polish Army. A pity neither the British nor the French people ever learned of those twin opinions. Weygand said the Polish Army was of no military value because of its inadequate tactical equipment and its incompetent leadership. He did not rank the Belgian army very highly either; he thought it was weakened by the political differences between the Walloons and the Flemings. He said the British Army would not count for much, but in his opinion the British Fleet would play a decisive rôle.

Where Weygand most misled the French Government and the people and helped dig the grave of the French Third Republic was when he so seriously misrepresented the power of Nazi Germany. Here it must be told why he so acted.

He admired Hitler because of the advantages he believed Hitler's policy would give the Roman Catholics in their fight against Communism.

It is not my intention to attempt to re-tell the tale of the 'Two Hundred Families' who were supposed to rule France until the arrival of the 'Popular Front', but it must be recalled that the fifteen 'Regents' of the Bank of France were recruited from those interlocking 'Two Hundred Families' and those 'Regents' were powerful men who made and unmade French Governments. To a man they backed General Weygand and his cohorts. They did not want war. According to them it was Britain who was forcing France towards a war in which she had no interest. Presently I shall come to the French people themselves, the crazed, dazed French people, who had been told so many things that they did not know what to believe; should they believe all or nothing? But as France came really close to war, in the summer of 1939, the people were not unhappy about anything. Behind the Maginot Line nothing could happen to them. There was magic in those two words. What of the Air Force? It was wonderful. So was the Navy; so were France's allies. If war came, the whole world with the exception of Italy and Japan and Russia would unite with France. The United States? Of course! The American Ambassador had said so, had he not?

Unfortunately, yes, he had.

The American Ambassador must have had an uneasy conscience when France fell. The part he played in the catastrophe was important.

William Bullitt, known to every junior member of his Paris staff as 'Bill', was a likeable, hail-fellow-well-met near-intellectual, who at one time in his career had been an enthusiastic 'pink' and whose first wife was the Russian-born Emma

Goldman, who supported the Bolsheviks. When President Roosevelt was elected President for the first time, he despatched his friend Bill Bullitt to Europe on a private fact-finding mission, and later, when America accorded diplomatic recognition to Soviet Russia, Bullitt was the first Ambassador to Moscow. Matters then did not turn out as Roosevelt hoped, so Bullitt was recalled and sent to Paris when the fate of France was in jeopardy. No one questioned Bullitt's sources of information; it was believed that he was the authentic voice of America. He told the French Government that there would be no war. Hitler was bluffing, he said. Alternatively, if there was a war, France had nothing to fear. The U.S.A. would be with her. France believed that because she wanted to believe it. What Bullitt had in mind there are no means of knowing. His 'information' was merely wishful thinking. He loved popularity and he was accorded that in full measure. He was host at fine parties held at the Paris American Embassy on the site of the former Jockey Club at the corner of the Place de la Concorde. But that was the only concord there was in France as the shadows cast by the coming event of war grew longer.

Edouard Daladier was Premier, but sniping at him from the French political undergrowth was Paul Reynaud, the man who eventually handed France over to Pétain for surrender.

Paul Reynaud was Minister of Justice, and later Minister of Finance. He had held Cabinet rank in several Governments; he belonged to no political party; in the Chamber of Deputies he sat as an Independent. In French political circles Reynaud was known as 'Mickey Mouse'; indeed, this little man who stands below average height bears a strong physical likeness to Walt Disney's cartoon. He was a lawyer, and a member of a wealthy family which derived its fortune from a department store in Mexico City. He speaks English and Spanish fluently. He was reputed to have many close contacts with the Paris Bourse, and was said to be a 'wizard of finance'. But he bore one close resemblance to his political enemy Edouard Daladier, whom he wished to replace as Premier. Both were subjected to what is called 'petticoat government'. His relations with women overshadowed his entire life, and for nearly twenty years, before he eventually became Premier, he was closely attached to the Countess Hélène de Portes, of whom the full story is told in the book *J'Accuse*. During his wartime leadership he was entirely under her domination. It was she who dictated French policy and it was Paul Reynaud who put that policy into execution from a small flat on the Place du Palais Bourbon, right at the back of the Chamber of Deputies.

The Countess was the daughter of a Marseilles civil engineer; she can best be described as being attractively ugly, and for years she had attracted men to her. Her marriage to the Count de Portes took place some years after she became the mistress of Paul Reynaud, but her marriage gave her the entrée both to Paris society and the circles of big business. According to political rumour she canvassed political support for several important French business interests.

Shortly after the fall of France she was motoring with Paul Reynaud on the French Riviera when they were involved in a motoring accident near St Maxime. The Countess sustained fatal injuries and died. Paul Reynaud escaped unhurt.

Edouard Daladier on his return from Munich had the second fright of his life; the first, as I have recorded, was when he ordered the soldiery to fire on the Stavisky rioters. Then in September, 1938, when his plane touched down at Le Bourget, and he saw the crowd, he thought it had come to lynch him. He blenched visibly, but the crowd consisted of the French opposite numbers of those who acclaimed Neville Chamberlain at Heston airport and Downing Street. What influence did the Munich Agreement have on the ultimate fall of France? None whatsoever. If France had gone to war then, as in 1939 or at any later date, the ultimate fate of France would have been the same. The French people at the time of Munich believed that war had been averted; Georges Bonnet and the bank that backed him multiplied the banknote-filled envelopes that were delivered safely into the hands of the chosen French journalists who wrote as they were told; included in the word 'journalist' is the word 'editor'. Even the *Petit Parisien* entered the camp of the appeasers of Hitler.

The *Petit Parisien* had the largest circulation in France; it also published the daily illustrated newspaper *Excelsior*, likewise with a large circulation. The *Petit Parisien* was founded by Senator Dupuy, who was succeeded by his son. When the son fell ill, he was ministered to by an American nurse, whom he married. He died in early middle age and left two sons. The widow carried on the newspaper while the sons were growing up, and they reached manhood in the days when France was drifting towards war; at that moment the policy of the *Petit Parisien* began to change. It would be difficult indeed to point to any Paris morning newspaper in the year 1939 and say unreservedly that its policy was not in some way or another tinged with a policy of appeasement. The very sad and distressing part of this story was that on the whole the readers of the French Press did not disagree with the reading material offered them. It was at this time that the anti-British sentiments began to creep in.

It began with the belief, fostered by Georges Bonnet and Pierre Laval, that Neville Chamberlain was in the hands of British Jews who wanted war. That sentiment grew stronger and stronger; there seemed to be no way of replying to those rumours. The second part of the story that followed hard on the heels of the first was that the British Government was putting pressure on the French Government to fall into line with British foreign policy. Already a part of the French Press was asking its readers: 'Do you wish to die for Czechoslovakia?' Unwittingly the British Government stepped up this anti-British propaganda. That was when the British Government made itself responsible for sixty per cent of the costs France might incur in a war with Germany. This stupid piece of generosity was not received with any gratitude; on the contrary, the French people said in effect: 'There you are then, you see, what did I tell you; Britain will fight to the last

Frenchman!' The French people really believed that Britain would pay France to fight and stay out of the war herself.

Otto Abetz, Hitler's representative in France, was married to a very clever Frenchwoman, who ably supported her husband in his campaign to undermine France. Abetz, at the time he was expelled from France—to return later in triumph to Vichy—spent literally millions of francs buying Senators and Deputies; he and his wife were on terms of close friendship with the Marquise de Uzès and the Comtesse de Portes. The Abetzs assiduously attended the *soirées* at both the women's homes, and mingled with the people they most desired to meet and influence. Their siren song was simple: a newspaper peer was singing it in Britain without it costing the Nazis a penny, but in France it was costly. The burden of the song paid tribute to Hitler's 'sincerity'. He did not want war, not he; he merely wanted to crush Communism, and all the wealthy French people and all those who hoped to be wealthy signified their approval in the usual way. But not all the bankers asked for money in order to be converted to the Hitler creed; by no means. Willy Somerset Maugham has his own story of a Paris banker friend who went to stay with him in his villa on Cap Ferrat when France was only a few steps from war. The banker had business dealings with Germany, and he was in close touch with the French Foreign Office. He told Somerset Maugham that German businessmen would be ruined by war and were strongly in favour of peace. He agreed there had been scares both in Germany and France, but Hitler, he said, did not want war; if Britain and France had been firmer at Munich, Hitler would have given way; if Britain and France had stood firm when Hitler had marched into Prague, Hitler would have withdrawn. Hitler had twice bluffed Britain and France, but now they were going to bluff him!

If responsible citizens like this Paris banker had such views, what could the French populace believe? They, as I said, believed just what they wanted to believe, and what they wanted to believe was that there would be no war; but if there was war, why, all the same, haven't we got the Maginot Line? *Eh bien alors!* So the fourteenth of July in 1939 came and went and there was dancing in the streets and the military procession down the Avenue des Champs Elysées passed the grandstand on which stood President Albert Lebrun and generals, admirals and Cabinet ministers, and a squadron of French military aircraft, one of the few capable of taking the air, flew from France across England, and over South Wales.

Eh bien alors!

Chapter IV

IT IS SO EASY to find one's way about in Paris, and so difficult in both London or New York, or so I have always found; in Paris when you are looking for a house number, and in Paris they *do* number the houses so that one can see the numbers, all one has to do is to remember that the numbers begin at the end of the streets nearest to the Seine. True, the Seine meanders much, yet what was more pleasant than meandering with it? But Paris more than any city I know is really nothing more than a collection of villages, twenty of them, and when you get to know them, or some of them, you form an affection for your *quartier* or village, and do not want to leave it. After many years of living in Chantilly, I moved to the Left Bank of the Seine, to the Quai de Javel, and happily lived my life there. I meandered; I even travelled in many foreign lands, but inevitably I returned to my village on the Seine; up in the rickety lift to my flat on the third floor with its windows overlooking the widest Parisian boulevard, the river Seine.

What was I doing in France throughout the setting of the scenes I have been describing? When I terminated, on my own volition, my service with the Beaverbrook newspapers, whose

Paris Correspondent I had been for twenty years, I established myself as an author and magazine writer, covering the world from Paris; not sitting peacefully on my rear but using the French capital as a base from whence to go here and there as news-features bubbled up like fish rising in a river; the fact that I was now writing, as I am still writing, a weekly commentary on foreign affairs, made those journeys all the more necessary, but I was always seeking new pastures wherein to graze.

The late C. B. Cochran had commissioned me to write a stage version of *Vanity Fair*; we had Lady Diana Cooper, the famous Diana Manners, in mind for the party of Becky Sharp. It was to have been a spectacular piece, opening with the Duchess of Richmond's ball in Brussels on the eve of the Battle of Waterloo. Lady Diana had played the part of the Nun in Cochran's production of *The Miracle*. But I doubted my ability to write a play solo, so I invited the collaboration of a man skilled in the art of the theatre; in the year 1939 'collaborator' had a less sinister sound that it achieved a very little later. Philip Carr was my choice; Carr was a son of the playwright Comyns Carr and was himself of the theatre; in previous years he had 'run' the English Theatre in Paris and was now the Paris Correspondent of the London *Observer*. Then one morning I was opening my English mail and found a letter from Cochran saying he could not proceed with the play owing to what he called 'unsettled conditions in London'.

It was all very pleasant being well informed about French politicians and generals and to know what was going on behind the French scene, but, come to think of it, that was remote and impersonal; this Cochran letter was highly personal. 'Unsettled conditions'! Was that a synonym for war? If so, what was war going to mean to *me*? I was just over the active service age limit, yet there were many things I might do for England, I thought in my carefree way; but my roots being deep in France, I fear I never dreamed that anything that I might do for England could in any way be unconnected with France.

Right down inside me I had always believed that in a second war with Germany, if the Germans again invaded, France would never emerge victorious, although, despite what I knew of corruption and defeatism, I did not really visualise defeat for France. That was a state of mind difficult, I know, to explain. Unwittingly I must have suffered from the Maginot Line complex.

I called up my collaborator, Philip Carr, who lived across the river in aristocratic Auteuil, and told him the bad news. But Carr was not much moved; he stressed the just-published new that Stalin had dismissed Maxim Litvinov, whom both of us had known at the Geneva meetings of the League of Nations; Stalin had replaced Litvinov with Molotov. Our conversation grew more and more mournful. When I hung up the receiver I walked over to another study window, the third, the one I did not like at all. Of the two I have mentioned, one looked directly across the river, the other up river, but the third looked down and across the Seine into Billancourt and the Renault factories. Latterly I had avoided that window as, metaphorically speaking, one avoids the windows of life that have an outlook on to unpleasant things. This third window's outlook told me plainly enough that if war and German planes came, there right opposite would be a main target, and life on the Quai de Javel would be highly unpleasant. But the lease of the flat did not expire until October, 1939, and then... ? So I would have to secure a line of retreat. My mind is a one-track one perhaps, which no doubt was why I immediately thought of a return to the forest, to Chantilly. I am a Free-mason, a member of Grand Lodge, which had, until the Germans came, a British branch Lodge in Chantilly, under-ground in reality, far enough from the vicarage of the English church to be beyond the confines of consecrated ground and so conformed to the rules of Freemasonry. I had a number of friends, some of them fellow Masons, among the British colony, about two hundred and fifty strong, in Chantilly; mostly people connected with horse-racing, upon which I do not look as an ungodly sport. So to Chantilly I hied myself, and found a five-roomed cottage, extremely ugly, in the Bois St Denis, right opposite the forest. It seemed so wonderfully peaceful. The landlord was a very, very old ex-jockey turned trainer and retired. His name, William Barker; he would not sell me the cottage, but he papered, distempered and painted it, put in running hot and cold water, and an ambassadorial bathroom, and rented it to me for £28 a year. Peace to his memory. He had an only daughter, a masterful woman, who spoke no English, and who was the widow of Chantilly's leading chemist, and signed herself Madame Lhuiller-Barker.

When, as I shall relate, the Germans came, she defied them, and was one of the few women of Chantilly who did, alas.

I did not want to leave my village on the Seine, but the signs and the portents of war were unmistakable; yet I hung on. Now various 'classes' of conscripts were called to the colours, retained for a while in barracks and billets and then sent home, disgruntled to a man. Those in barracks complained that there was a lack of army boots; that was quite true; men had to parade in their own footgear. Those in billets complained of the food; they had to get their womenfolk to get them food; and the farmers could not supply them with straw on which to sleep in their barns. That was true, too. Worst of all, this did not happen once or twice, but several times; each time, naturally, the conscripts grumbled more. 'This dirty Government, what do they think they are?' The bosses of the office and factory workers who were called up 'for nothing' complained because they said it was ruining their business, and the farmers whose hands had to go said that the farm work was going to the devil. People were told to go to their local town halls and procure gas-masks; they waited hours and went home empty-handed because the gas-masks had been ordered from Czecho-slovakia, and since Hitler had annexed that country the deliveries of gas-masks had ceased.

47

What heart-searchings I had; should I 'close up the shop' and go to Britain? I did not say 'back to Britain'; I could not; I had come from Britain years before and had settled in France; France was home, not Britain. Yet I felt the latent but rising —what shall I say?—not hate, but dislike of Britain that could now be sensed more than heard.

I offered my services to the French Army as an interpreter and waited for a reply. Eventually I received a curt note from the Military Headquarters at Senlis, near Chantilly, saying that if my credentials were in order I would be allowed to become a private in an infantry regiment. I joined a friend and neighbour, Donald Watson, and drove with him and his wife to Trouville, to attend the yearling sales at neighbouring Deauville. Both resorts were packed out. Who said war was near? Watson trained racehorses for a rich Englishwoman, a Mrs Cartwright. On her behalf he purchased three yearlings for several thousand pounds. Nine months later they were slaughtered and sold to horse butchers.

I returned to Paris on August 28th, 1939, and two days later I moved from Paris to Chantilly. That I felt was a security measure. What a fool I was!

Paris had a bad attack of jitters. For forty-eight hours the city seethed with rumours of a sudden German aerial attack. In the midst of this panic I secured a lorry and a driver, plus two men not yet mobilised, and at dawn and all day long that day I helped to carry furniture, beds, divans, carpets, rugs, pictures and three thousand books, all the time thinking any minute now the bombs may begin to fall. My cottage was now so stuffed up that moving around was difficult. There was an air of breathlessness hanging over the countryside as I drove back from Paris again that night. It was a beautiful starlit night, but it seemed all wrong; instead of the peaceful pastoral scene there should have been a Wagnerian night of heavy roaring thunder and flashes of lightning. Came the morning, the dawn of another lovely day; the dew on the grass; the crisp sound of racehorses being walked past the cottage, and in the evening the lowing of cattle; the sweet smell of mint as dusk turned into night.

On September 1st three men came to fix my bookcases: a father and two sons. They worked fast, because the sons had to go to their regimental depot the same afternoon. In the village streets there were men carrying brown *musettes*, with a bottle of wine and the end of a crusty loaf sticking out, trudging to the station en route to the war. Their fathers had gone to their war in 1914 singing and shouting: '*à Berlin!*' Now they were sullen, 'fed up'. They seemed bewildered, and no wonder.

Next day I noticed men digging trenches in the forest just across the road from my front garden gate; they told me they were air-raid shelters. It was that day I realised my cottage was but a few yards from the main railway line from Amiens to Paris. Every day now I noticed the town crier on his bicycle; he dismounted, played a roll on his drum and read a notice to a small crowd of English stable-boys and French school-children. Each notice concluded with the phrase: '*Qu'on se le dise, le Maire Semiand.*' One always expected some world-shattering proclamation, but it was always merely something either about a lost dog or a found brooch. In the rue de Conétable, Chantilly's main street, I met 'Ton-ton' ('Unkey'), the fat and jovial driver of the municipal dustcart; there would be no war, he told me, he had it on the best authority from some of those big bonnets up in Paris. Everything would arrange itself. Then on Sunday September 3rd I heard that Chamberlain was going to speak at 11 o'clock. He would announce war, I was told, but I still thought in terms of miracles, and fully believed he would make some startling announcement. I switched on the wireless and heard him say we were in a 'state of war'. I broke down and wept, but all at once I began to juggle with words; did a 'state of war' mean the same thing as being at war? And France, what of France? I clung to the wishful thought that some eleventh-hour miracle might emerge from the fact that France at our eleventh hour was not at war. I suppose I was not alone with that wishful thought that Sunday morning.

I drove up to Paris that afternoon, and heard of the air-raid alarm in London. Paris railway stations were still full of men called up and going away, and women standing about crying. Out in the streets people stood looking up at the empty blue sky. I went down to the Foreign Office on the Quai d'Orsay. There was a crowd outside, wondering what was going on inside. Four hours had passed since Britain went to war, and France had said no word. The early editions of the evening papers appeared, and there were plenty of white open spaces; the censors were already at work; people filled in the blanks with rumours: Mussolini was working for peace; it would be all right; Chamberlain, the sly old devil, had just made a gesture, that was all, just a gesture. Everything will be fixed. Chamberlain is coming to Paris; no, Daladier is going to London; no, both of them are going to Rome. I went and had a drink; several drinks. At 5.30 I heard the news. For half an hour France had been at war.

The streets of Paris were dull now. People came back from the races at Longchamps, bought the papers and sat down on still sunny café terraces and read the news. There was no excitement.

There were still plenty of British tourists in Paris and now I remarked that people speaking English were looked at curiously. I drove back to Chantilly, fetched my friends the Watsons, and went to the Hotel Condé bar for a drink. Nothing had changed there; the usual cosmopolitan crowd, but it was quiet; Georges the barman in his white jacket was playing cards with Charlie Elliot the jockey and two Frenchmen. When I went outside it was dark and I noticed that it was darker than usual, then I remembered that there was a war on. I went back to my cottage, switched on the wireless and listened to the news. It seemed that the Poles were doing marvellously well; they had bombed Berlin! I undressed and went to bed and switched on my bedside wireless. There were more victories; the Poles were still doing well; Danzig was holding fast. Then I switched off the wireless and the lights and went to sleep.

The sirens woke me up. I dressed and went out across the road to the forest and looked at the air-raid trenches; they looked very damp, but they had some people in them. I decided to walk about in the forest until the 'all-clear' sounded. The next morning I discovered that I was living in the 'Zone of the Armies'. Technically one had to have a special permit to go to and from Paris. In the first war the Germans had reached Chantilly but stayed about a day only. Now one could not telephone to Paris without a permit; if one talked English one was immediately cut off.

Before the week was out there was no coffee in the shops; no oil either, and hardly any soap. I went to the Town Hall to obtain my petrol ration; I asked for forty litres a month; the employee answered: 'Don't be silly, that's not enough!'

The days dragged on; there was no action; the newspapers had many blank spaces and the German war communiqués were not published. Every night now the air-raid siren sounded and I heard the German planes passing over the cottage, but no bombs were dropped. The French anti-aircraft guns fired and I heard the patter of shrapnel-like pellets on the roof.

Up in Paris the so-called balloon barrage consisted of six balloons. *Chez moi* in Chantilly, the gallops where the horses used to train in the early morning were now the airfield, on which stood a number of elderly aircraft. The airmen regaled the local ladies with tales of their imaginary exploits every night over Berlin.

My life was very boring now. In the mornings I worked in the garden and in the afternoons I dictated to my dictaphone, which a little later was nearly my undoing, but I felt a great need for action. I drove up to Paris and went to the British Military Attaché's office, where I found a notice saying the office was closed to all those seeking employment. Then again I thought of going to London. There was now a very marked

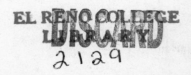
EL REÑO COLLEGE LIBRARY DISCARD
2129

defeatist attitude in Chantilly, and the English population were getting very dirty looks from the local people. Within the first week of the war there had been a rumour that all the Chantilly men had been killed; actually, as I learned later, one man had died of pneumonia. But there is no doubt that at that time German agents were already very active in Chantilly. There was one man, who had taken quite a large house in the middle of the village not very long before the war. He claimed to be British of Swiss descent. He was extremely anti-British. He used to go round visiting the English racehorse trainers and spread rumours about Britain's unpreparedness for war. Then there was a French prince married to an American woman, who was very pro-German. Another person who came under great suspicion, not particularly from myself, but from other people in Chantilly, was an Alsatian woman dentist, whose husband had been mobilised and had gone to Syria. The French people asked themselves why this woman and another, a friend of hers, were always seen around with French officers. Then there appeared a very interesting case, a fair-haired English-speaking person who claimed that he was a Dutchman. His job, as I shall explain later, was to keep an eye on the large number of German and Austrian Jewish refugees who were now pouring into Chantilly. They had been driven out of Paris by the French authorities.

As the French were not disposed, so it seemed, to make use of my volunteered wartime services, I thought I would try what I could do with my own countrymen, and having failed to contact the British Military Attaché, I went to see an old friend, Major Geoffrey Courtney, who was then British Passport Officer in Paris; he is the son of a famous Victorian journalist, W. L. Courtney of the *Daily Telegraph*. It was known to me that British passport officers were frequently connected with one of the Army Intelligence services; however, that is one of the things one does not mention in conversation. I asked Courtney if it was likely that my services would be useful to the War Office.

'Of course', he said simply. 'When can you go to London?'

I left for London the same night. I had to travel via Le Havre and Southampton, across the Channel, with the French-Canadian crew of a tanker that had been sunk in the Mediterranean. I woke up in the Solent and saw what looked like a school of grey aerial porpoises floating in an azure sky. It was my first sight of a real balloon barrage. Courtney had asked me where I could be contacted in London, and I had told him at the Royal Automobile Club. They had no room for me there, so I secured a lodging in nearby Ryder Street. And waited. And waited. My friend David Walker has told in *Lunch with a Stranger* how his wartime secret adventures began at the R.A.C.; so did mine, but not over lunch; a stranger looked in on me for a dish of tea. It happened like this.

While I was waiting in London to be contacted by some British master spy, I looked up some of my editorial friends. I told Frank Owen, who was editing the *Evening Standard*, of the differences between the 'blue-out' of Paris and the 'black-out' of London. In Jermyn Street a harlot stole the handkerchief out of my breast-pocket while I was stumbling along over sandbags on my way to Ryder Street. In Paris even the 'angels of the night' looked blue. The upshot of the conversation was that I wrote a piece for the *Evening Standard* called 'The Tale of Two Cities', and if I had unwittingly attacked the wartime policy of Chamberlain I could hardly have caused more controversy. But when all that died down, there I was, still sitting at the R.A.C., waiting.

On September 20th I cabled Courtney in Paris asking him to hurry matters up for me. In the Club I found friends whom I had known in foreign parts, and who had hurried to London to offer their services, but, like me, they were waiting. While I waited I received disquietening news from my Chantilly cottage. Two police inspectors had called and made enquiries about me. They exhibited a picture of me which appeared to be a tracing of my passport picture. They made the rounds of my study and closely examined the books I had written; then they said they were investigating a report that I had been seen around Chantilly 'wearing Nazi uniform'. That made me laugh, because I saw the explanation at once. A couple of years previously Roland Wild and I had spent the winter in the Liberian jungle, obtaining material for a book. We wore khaki shirts and khaki shorts. I still had a whole stack of those shirts and used to wear them in the country; khaki is a shade of brown; the Nazis wore brown shirts; hence the Nazi uniform. But the parting question of the police was devastating: was it true that I had gone to London to become a member of the British Intelligence Service? I was drafting a reply to Chantilly when I was called to one of the Club telephones; a mysterious call, said to be from the War Office. Would I call there the following morning?

The lift that seemed to be a blood-brother of the one in the Printing House Square office of *The Times*, it was so frightfully shaky, took me up to the top floor, where I was led along a corridor and shown into a room that contained an iron bedstead, a table and two chairs. Also a dapper little man wearing a blue suit. His opening phrase was: 'Let's get right down to brass tacks', but although I was more than willing, we certainly journeyed nowhere.

I really do not know what I expected. I had no aptitude for spying, so far as I knew, but I did suppose that as I could speak French and German fluently and correctly, and had travelled in Europe very extensively, and had spent years interviewing people of all kinds, from charladies, through the ranks of statesmen, up to the realms of reigning monarchs, my services for the purpose of compiling information concerning trends of opinion in foreign countries might be found useful. But was I wrong! I talked; I answered questions. Then I was told I would be convoked again.

Nothing happened for several days. Then came another telephone call; the person who had met me recently would be calling on me at the Club that afternoon. I entertained him to tea and Dundee cake. This time there was a probing examination of me: what countries did I know best; how well did I

54

know France, Switzerland and Italy; did I speak French, German and Italian? I was able to say I spoke the first two named languages fluently. Then, whom did I know in those aforementioned countries? That took me aback; I knew numerous people, my journalistic contacts for years. Names, please. Certainly not. Journalists never disclose the names of their contacts. Tea was sipped silently for a full three minutes. Then: 'How much money do you want?'

'M-m-money?' I spluttered. 'I'm not asking for any money; I assumed that my expenses would be paid, I don't want anything more.' Oh dear, oh dear; if only I had been warned. Since then, over the years, British agents, more or less secret, have told me in words of one syllable what sort of fool I was. It seems that my innocent reply would indicate that I was no doubt in the pay of an enemy. Actually, what the man in the blue suit said as he stood up and thanked me for the tea was: 'Goodbye, you'll be hearing from us.' I did hear, about a week later. There came a letter, saying there was nothing that could be offered me.

I was furious about the waste of my time and money. Leslie Hore-Belisha was still Secretary of State for War; I had been at school with him, and later he was my colleague on the staff of the *Daily Express*. I wrote him a note, telling him what had happened to me. There came back a letter advising me to return to Paris at once, and promising I should be posted to the first British Military Mission sent abroad. Then other things began to happen to me.

Chapter V

ALL THROUGH my journalistic life I had had to deal with red tape, but never did I expect to find it barring my way forward as it did one day in October, 1939, when I wanted to return to my home in France and there wait for the fulfilment of the promise Leslie Hore-Belisha had made to me. I had my still valid British passport, but as I had been travelling so much, its pages were almost full up with many visas; therefore I thought it would be a good idea if I went along to the Passport Office and asked for a new passport. I had held passports for many years, and each one stated that France was my elected domicile, yet now, the passport officer who interviewed me seemed extremely suspicious. He wanted to know why I wanted to go to France, and naturally I told him that I merely wanted to go home. When I said that he asked me why I wanted to go home. I told him that I had been in London to try and get some job under the Government, but there was nothing doing, so I was going back to resume my profession of journalism. He pricked up his ears at that, and said that if I was a journalist I could not go to France unless I obtained the permission of the Ministry of Information. So I took a taxi to Senate House. There I explained my difficulty to a liveried doorkeeper, who produced a list of typewritten names; there seemed to be hundreds and hundreds of them. I ran my eye down the list and I did come across a name I knew, that of a journalist who for some years had served on the same newspaper as myself. I sent up my name, and in due course I was able to see him. He said he really did not know what he could do about the matter, but he suggested I should go and see a Mr Balfour, who was, it appeared, the head of the French Section. I had to wait an hour before I did see this gentleman, a young man with a black Café Royalist beard. He was paring his nails; so was his secretary. My entry into the office did not cause them to cease what they were doing, but I began to say why I wanted to go home. Mr Balfour shook his head sadly and said there was nothing he could do about it, but on a question of principle he would take the matter up with the Home Office. I could hardly believe what I heard, although I did ask how long this would take. Mr Balfour said it would take a few days. I had told Mr Balfour that I had commissions to write articles for the *Evening Standard* and the *Sphere*. A little later that afternoon I learned that Mr Balfour's office had been in touch by telephone with the editor of the *Evening Standard*; the editor had told him that he knew me quite well; what I had said was in point of fact completely true. But the editor of the *Evening Standard* was not very pleased about Mr Balfour, so he took up the matter himself by giving me a letter to the French Embassy, where I was granted a special visa, and what is more, I found myself accredited to French G.H.Q. Armed with those documents, the British Passport Office issued me a new passport, so at long last I was able to go home, to France.

The next morning, I noticed that the *Petit Parisien*, which had not yet entered the camp of the appeasers, had published a story about the retreat of General Gamelin's armies. According to the French newspaper, the retreat was not at all important. It was, however, with a very disturbed mind that I went back to Chantilly and began to work.

A few days later a dust-covered motor-car drew up in front of my cottage, a short fair-haired man alighted and came to the front door. My maid knocked and announced: '*La Police*'. The man came in and showed me his card. He was a police inspector from Amiens. I told him about the two detectives who had visited my house while I was in London. The Amiens inspector looked at his notebook and it was apparent that he had no record of the previous visit from the police. I showed him my newspaper credentials, and he appeared satisfied. As I was showing him to the door I asked him why I was so constantly under police notice. His reply was very disturbing. He said: 'There's somebody who is not a friend of yours, evidently.' I could not fathom the meaning of this, to me, cryptic remark. I ran through the people I knew in Chantilly, and until I came to the name of the man to whom I have already made reference, the strange person who had arrived just before the outbreak of war and taken a house in the centre of the town, I could think of nobody at all. I certainly had had a passage of arms with this man, when I knew that he was going round the English trainers and getting into conversation with them by asking questions about training horses, saying that possibly he would be purchasing some racehorses. That led to further visits, and on each occasion he managed to introduce statements derogatory to Britain. A few days later there was more evidence of disturbing happenings. A young Englishwoman I knew had gone to the local police station on some matter or other, and was kept waiting a very long time. She asked politely how much longer she would have to wait; the police inspector flew into a temper and screamed: 'Where do you think you are? You're not in England, you know!' The English girl replied quietly that if she had been in England, then she would have been treated politely. Then there came more trouble for me, personally.

I received a visit from one of the local gendarmes whom I knew well. He left a scrap of paper, what is known as a *convocation*, saying that I must report at once to the police station. I drove there; the gendarme who had called on me went on ahead. The inspector on duty told the gendarme: 'Take this man to the gendarmerie.' I drove on, while the gendarme pedalled behind my car. The gendarmerie was in a quiet road just behind Chantilly Castle. We went into the gendarmerie, where there were three very tall and good-looking gendarmes all wearing khaki uniforms. They went on talking and ignored me completely. This I knew was an old trick of the French police which they always adopt when they want to intimidate a suspect, so I asked after waiting a few minutes why I had been sent for. One of the gendarmes turned to me and asked: 'What's your nationality?' I handed him my passport without saying anything. He then said sternly: 'What's your nationality; what's your name?'

I pointed to my passport, which was in his hand, and told him that he would find all the information there. He answered with what was intended for sarcasm: 'I can't read.' I told him that it would be quite easy to read what was in the passport, because British passports were in English and in French. He glanced inside the passport, banged the covers between his hands and handed me back the document.

That was all I knew, and very little use it was to me. One could sense the rising hostility to the British. The days dragged on, but there was nothing to do but work and go to Paris occasionally. The French Ministry of Information was in the great big Hotel Continental, which I found full of young French officers, both in the army and navy. I had to search mighty hard to find the British section. Finally I discovered the late Philip Carr who, with his French wife, formed the link between the British Ministry of Information and the French. The Carrs were well guarded by two Anglo-French Boy Scouts, one with a fine moustache. Madame Carr was writing her cookery book. Carr asked me to do a series of five-minute broadcasts to be delivered from Paris to the B.E.F. I was to cover various aspects of French life. I asked Carr what time I would have to go on the air, and he replied: 'At six p.m.' I was very astonished and asked if the British troops would not at that hour be listening to the B.B.C. news from home. Carr said innocently: 'Oh, is there news at that time?' Then I went looking for the French censor of English mailed magazine articles. I found him in a dingy back bedroom. The censor looked very bored and surprised when I handed him an article for his perusal. I told him that the editor of the *Sphere* insisted that articles must be submitted to the French censor. Very bored, he wearily took the article from my hands. I had to provide him with a stamped addressed envelope; one never saw the articles again once they were handed in to the censor, unless they were passed, and then they duly appeared in the British publication for which they were intended. A few days later I was asked by a French literary agency if I would prepare an English version of a biography of André Maginot, which had just been written by a Madame Gauthier, who was Maginot's self-admitted mistress. André Maginot was the man who invented the Maginot Line. Then the same agent asked me if I would go in with him on preparing for the British market articles written by Otto Strasser. The agent, Paul Winkler, who had very useful friends in French high political circles, told me that the French Government was holding Strasser in reserve, to put in power in Germany as soon as Hitler fell. If this was truly their intention, most certainly the French Government was not wasting much money on Otto Strasser.

I kept an appointment with him in the small hotel in which he was living in the rue Monsieur le Prince. We sat in his small bedroom and talked German because he could not speak French, and his English was hardly noticeable. I found him very smug and complacent. He pretended to know everything that was happening inside Germany, but I doubted that very much indeed. While I was talking to Otto Strasser, I was thinking of another German who had been associated with Hitler. The man I had in mind was Fritz von Thyssen, who was living with his wife in great state at the expensive Hotel Crillon, whereas Otto Strasser, who had been Hitler's right-hand man when von Thyssen was his backer, had had to run for his life and reached Prague and was now living in this back bedroom in the small hotel on the Left Bank of Paris on a monthly subsidy of £28, which Winkler was paying him.

I recall that on that day and on other days when passing the terrace of the Café de la Paix, I invariably saw the Chantilly 'Dutchman' sitting in a circle surrounded by German and Austrian Jewish refugees. The Café de la Paix was their favourite meeting place, and it struck me as being more than curious that the 'Dutchman' was always among them, just as he was always among them in the little bar in Chantilly which they used to frequent. Hundreds of Jewish refugees had been turned out of Paris and had been told to go and live in Chantilly. I was convinced, although I confess that I did not have any proof whatsoever, that this alleged Dutchman was reporting on the conversations of those unfortunate refugees. In Paris at this time there were curious stories about Lord Beaverbrook. It was said that he was going to purchase the Paris evening newspaper *Paris Soir*, also that he had a plan to restore peace by getting the Duke of Windsor back to England. I suppose that in a country like France, where there was at that time a café society and where during wartime the newspapers were heavily censored, there was bound to be a great deal of rumour-mongering, but I am sure that there were more rumours spread around Paris during the last war than there ever were during the first war; most undoubtedly it was this rumour-mongering in Paris and the other cities that helped in no small measure to undo the morale of the French people.

I was eager to see some action, but there was certainly nothing going on on the war front, so I decided to go to Strasbourg to see if I could find a story there.

On the Rhine I found the French and the Germans fighting verbal battles; both had batteries of loudspeakers; the Germans talked in French and the French talked in German, and each side was broadcasting loudly propaganda lies to the other side. I recall the Germans telling the French how Britain was exploiting them, whereas the French were telling the Germans that the blockade was going to starve them to death. Of the two, I thought the Germans came out best, because the French so evidently did not like the British, so they were always open to a little malicious gossip. In Strasbourg itself it was difficult to believe that the French morale was high. The public was not aware that the whole of Upper Alsace had been evacuated. Strasbourg was like a city of the dead. Fly-blown cakes were in shuttered pastrycooks' shops; newspapers turning brown at the edges were to be seen behind the windows of closed-up kiosks. There was an air of sadness. One's footsteps echoed along the deserted streets. Occasionally I saw a householder accompanied to his door by the police. He entered, and came out again with bedding or household utensils. These he would load up on a handcart and wheel away towards the station. He had come back to Strasbourg with a special permit from the part of France where he was billeted. There was not a stray dog or cat to be seen; just marching soldiers, and a few policemen; that was all. Then when I returned to Paris I found more trouble awaited me.

Still another gendarme called at my cottage and said that he had come to investigate an accident in which I had been involved with my car. I asked him when, and the day he said the accident was supposed to have happened was the day when I was on my way back from Strasbourg. He asked if he could look at the car. I sent the servant out to the garage with him. She told me that as soon as he saw the car he did not look to see whether there were any marks or dents on the bonnet or wings, he just looked inside the car and searched for a wireless transmitter. Such a thing I had never possessed in my life.

Well, the clouds were growing ever thicker, and my situation, my personal situation, was growing more and more dismal. I could not obtain a wartime job, while all around me the waves of anti-British hostility were rising higher and higher. There were veiled criticisms in the newspapers, but it was in the shops and the cafés and the French homes that Britain was the target for open attack: blame for pushing France into war; blame for doing nothing while France was at war. The French people never did realise that war was inevitable, but as a British subject devoted to France I knew only too well as the first wartime spring arrived that, just as war was inevitable, so was defeat inevitable for France.

BOOK TWO

Chapter I

IT SEEMED THAT my friend Leslie Hore-Belisha had either forgotten his promise or else he was unable to implement it; I heard nothing from him, and I was desperate about getting some sort of a wartime job. Chantilly reeked with rumours. An Englishwoman told me that there had been five hundred German planes over Chantilly, taking photographs. She claimed she had seen them herself. But perhaps the best of all was a little Cockney stable boy who said to his boss: 'Garn! 'Itler cawn't win; up to now 'es only been up against platers. Now 'e's up against class!'

Then I received a letter written on House of Commons notepaper from a Colonel Baldwin Webb saying he was founding an Anglo-French Ambulance Corps. He offered me a job as a driver of an ambulance; the pay was to be five francs a day. I declined his offer, saying that the pay was inadequate. Some little time later I learned that the Colonel had been drowned while crossing the Atlantic.

It is very difficult to set down in cold blood the feeling of frustration that was current all around me. It became known to me that Jean Chiappe who, as I have already related, was once Paris Prefect of Police, had supplied von Ribbentrop with secret information concerning the loves and intrigues and financial dealings of prominent French politicians. Then came a real bombshell; I never knew whether it found an echo in Britain. Premier Edouard Daladier said: 'We shall not take the initiative, but we shall return blow for blow.' This seemed to make it perfectly clear that France, at that time at any rate, had no thought of launching an offensive against the Germans. The plan appeared to be for France to sit tight behind the Maginot Line. It was shortly after this speech that it became known that Daladier's days were numbered.

Chantilly now received more and more German and Austrian refugees. There were so many that there was no accommodation for them and they were put into unheated concentration camps around the countryside. I used to see some of the women, wearing fur coats, washing their linen in the municipal wash-house, or sometimes in the Oise canal. Then shortly after Christmas came the news that Leslie Hore-Belisha had been dropped from the Cabinet. Now where was my job? But the news of Leslie's passing from office was well received in Paris. Army officers expressed their pleasure that he had been dismissed, because they knew that the ex-Secretary for War had been responsible for the dismissal of a number of British officers. Others, civilians, were heard to say: 'That's one Jew less.'

I filled in time by going up to Paris to obtain material from Otto Strasser, and then to Paul Winkler's office in the rue de la Paix to obtain material from Maginot's mistress. When I had a little time to spare I went to the *Marianne* office in the Avenue des Champs Elysées. Pierre Wolf, the 'grey eminence' of Paternôtre, was always amusing. He was contemptuous of everything but women and money. Once a week he used to take the members of his staff down to his country house near Chartres and win back their wages at poker. Then, in the middle of March, Daladier's Government fell. Paul Reynaud became Prime Minister. At the same time I learned for the first time that whereas Marshal Foch had been a real commander-in-chief of the Allied armies in France, in the second war General Gamelin was merely a 'consultative' commander-in-chief; he had the power to advise General Gort what to do, but he had no power to order him to do it. Therefore the B.E.F. in France was completely autonomous. But at that time

I do not suppose there were a thousand French people who knew the truth.

At the end of March, at long last I received a letter from the British Military Attaché's office in Paris to say that my application of the previous September had been passed on and I was to call. I went to Paris, where I learned from French journalists that Daladier was already sorry that he had given up office and was beginning to start a political war to bring down Reynaud and regain the premiership. At the same time there was a move on foot to displace Gamelin from the High Command. There was also a strong French military faction that was trying to unseat Gort. His statement the previous January that Britain had 'turned the corner', a statement made at a moment when Britain had not done any fighting, was received with derisive laughter in French military quarters. There were rumours in Paris that the Germans were about to invade Holland and Belgium, but nobody seemed to believe it.

On my birthday I called at the Military Attaché's office, where I discovered that the man who had sent for me was Captain Gielgud (later Colonel Gielgud), a brother of the famous London actor. There was just a little conversation, but I did not seem to have carried my application any further. I returned to Chantilly, where I went on waiting. There was now complete apathy everywhere; nobody seemed in any way keen to get on with the war.

I went on working and waiting until the first week in May, when I was sent for once again to go to the British Military Attaché's office, and there I was told that there would be a job for me and I would be notified at any minute now, but the next day when I returned to my cottage, I switched on the wireless and heard that Holland and Belgium had been invaded. In the middle of this tragedy there was a note of high comedy. General Gamelin's order of the day said he had been expecting the attack since last October. What had happened during those seven months it was difficult even to guess at, as it became known very soon that the mines placed beneath the Belgian bridges did not go into action because the switches had been removed, and as for Holland, the Dutch had refused to allow the dykes to be opened, because they said that sea water would ruin their land. So they had the Germans instead.

A day or two later I took my car out; it was Sunday afternoon; I drove along the road towards Paris. I had a thermos of tea with me, and I sat down by the roadside. Although it was only twenty-four hours since the Germans had invaded Belgium, I was amazed to see a number of motor-cars hurtling along the road towards Paris, and on the back of each car was a big 'B' in red letters. The cars obviously belonged to wealthy Belgians. Idly I counted more than fifty of such cars. There was practically no news of any fighting. Over Chantilly the planes were now coming by day and by night, but they dropped no bombs, so nobody took any notice of them; seldom the sirens sounded, and very often the anti-aircraft guns did not open up until long after the German planes had passed overhead.

Then on Whit Sunday, 1940, Chantilly was bombed for the first time; and I was placed under arrest by the R.A.F. Intelligence Service.

I was in a bath when my servant knocked at the door with the now familiar words: '*La Police*'. She said two gendarmes were asking for me; I put on a bath-gown and I went outside. There were two gendarmes armed with carbines; they said I had to go with them. I dressed quickly. In a black car outside were two more. A small crowd had gathered. I asked what the matter was; all I could learn was that I had to go with the gendarmes. They marched me out and pushed me into the car while the crowd hissed. I sat between the two armed gendarmes; we drove to the end of the avenue and then turned left on to the main Amiens-Paris road for about a hundred yards; then the car entered the garden of a large house opposite the Terrain des Aigles, which in pre-war days was where the race-horses were trained but, as I have told, since the war began it had been an airfield. There I was told to get out of the car, which then drove away. I stood waiting until a young man came out of the house. He was in R.A.F. uniform. I was greatly surprised. He asked for my passport, which fortunately I happened to have in my pocket. I gave it to him and I asked him what was the matter. He told me that I was suspected. I asked him of what I was suspected, and he replied: 'Of everything and nothing.' I told the officer that I was about to be appointed to an Intelligence post; I asked if he would call up the Paris Embassy on the telephone. He said he would, but for the moment he looked through my passport and saw that I had several dozen visas. He asked me why I was 'always travelling'. I explained that I was a journalist and that I travelled on journalistic missions.

While he was talking another car containing two R.A.F. officers drove into the garden. The officer who had been questioning me then walked back into the house and I was left standing in the garden in the boiling sun for an hour. Then a British despatch rider came in from the world outside and parked his motor-cycle. I did not want to begin a conversation because I had been told that I was under suspicion and I did not think it politic to talk to anybody. But the young motorcyclist was over-charged with conversation. He told me how things were going 'up at the front' and so on. Then just as he was telling me about the retreat of the British Army, the fairhaired officer returned and said he was unable to get the Embassy on the telephone. He told me that I could go home, but he would have to retain my passport. I said to him then: 'If you really want to investigate something that has great need of investigation, why don't you investigate those four strange Germans who are living openly in the rue Blanche?' He jotted down some notes of what I said and then he commented: 'The French don't collaborate.' Perhaps a little later his words would have borne a different and more sinister meaning.

I returned home and found I was late for lunch. Just as I was sitting down to eat there was a series of very loud explosions; the cottage shook like a jelly. The explosions continued for four or five minutes. Then there was a dead silence. Five minutes later I heard the wail of the sirens giving the air-raid alarm. Nine bombs had fallen round my cottage; forty had fallen on the village of Chantilly. Seven people were killed and a number of racehorses had to be slaughtered. The Germans had been trying to bomb the railway and the airfield, and had missed both. In the afternoon I went out and found that the R.A.F. had persuaded the French authorities to arrest the four Germans to whom I had called attention. They had arrested the two women and one of the men; the other man was shot as he tried to escape over a wall.

Now it became known to me from French newspaper sources that General Georges, who would have had command of the French Armies if he had not been so severely wounded in Marseilles when King Alexander of Yugoslavia was assassinated, was fighting a private war of his own with General Gamelin; each general was in command of a group of armies, but their direction was not co-ordinated. Everybody seemed to be pinning their hopes on General Giraud, who commanded the Seventh Army and who had the British on his right flank.

On paper, the Anglo-French forces sounded as if they were very strong, and perhaps it was on this account that it was difficult for the French to understand what was happening at the front. Once again, it came to my knowledge from newspaper offices that on the north-east front the French had only ninety-five bombers, but, so I was informed, two-thirds of them were valueless. The French Army in this sector had four hundred and twenty fighting planes. Then the Germans attacked on the Meuse, where the bridges were mined, yet when the sappers went to blow them up they found that the fuses had been removed, just as had occurred in Belgium. The French Ninth Army, under the command of General Gorap, was rushed up in lorries to defend the passages of the Meuse, but the troops, who consisted of Spahis and Territorials, refused to alight from the vehicles. This incidentally was the

French Army's first experience of dive-bombing. The Army broke and quit and the Germans crossed the Meuse with ease and with only slight losses. They transported their light and heavy tanks with speed. The heavy tanks crossed the un-damaged bridges, and the light tanks were loaded on to rubber pontoons. French and Belgian agents working for the Germans had already indicated the shallow parts of the river. I did not know how much London knew of what was happening, but I did think that a great deal of what was happening must have been received. I was undeceived when I received a letter from Jesse Heitner, editor of the *Sphere*, who wrote to tell me at this moment that as there was no action in France, he must suspend my articles until he and I had an opportunity to have a talk!

Chapter II

THERE WAS A FRENCHMAN named Ferdonnet who now, in 1940, was doing more to assist Germany to defeat France than could be imagined. I still know nothing about him except that he was a Frenchman who worked for the Germans and became an announcer at Radio Stuttgart, from whence he wrought havoc in France from the beginning of the war and until France surrendered. His knowledge of propaganda values was fantastic; while the French soldiery waited in idleness for something to happen, Ferdonnet told them how they were being sacrificed in the interests of Capitalism. I do not suggest that the *poilus* cared so much about that, but when he told them that while they were in the line the British in the rear were going to bed with their wives, that was something else entirely. That made the French soldiers think hard, and when there was perhaps some evidence of an isolated case, then the general idea spread. The ground was prepared for the second stage of propaganda.

The Germans issued a poster called the 'Bath of Blood'; these posters were dropped from planes and circulated through agents behind the French lines. The poster was in four sections. The first picture showed a French and a British soldier standing on the edge of a blood-filled pond; the second picture showed both soldiers preparing to jump in, but the third picture showed that the Frenchman had dived in alone, leaving the Tommy standing on the bank. In the fourth picture the Frenchman was up to his neck in blood, and the Englishman was walking away laughing. This, however, was by no means the sum total of Ferdonnet's activities.

The French agents working for the Germans supplied Ferdonnet with the most minute details of French activities; things that could not possibly have been known to anyone outside various small circles. For instance, to my certain knowledge, he broadcast that a certain French division in a western front sector was going to be moved, one half by road and the other half by rail. The officers knew nothing at all about such a troop movement, but twenty-four hours later the order came from corps headquarters, exactly as Ferdonnet had forecast. On another occasion he warned a corps commander over the air from Stuttgart that the wives and mistresses of officers in his command were in the habit of joining the officers in nearby towns for the weekend. The corps commander made his enquiries and the information proved to be correct.

While such things were happening at the front, I was sitting in my study listening to the B.B.C. nine o'clock news one evening in the third week of May, 1940, when I heard a tinkle of the bell on my garden gate. I went out to investigate; it was pitch dark. Through the bars of the gate I could see dimly the outline of a man wearing a cap. I asked him what he wanted. 'Open up', he commanded. 'This is a military search party.' I unlocked the gate and immediately the civilian rushed past me; he was followed by a French aviation officer and four men; all of them except the civilian were carrying revolvers in their hands. The seven of us went into the cottage. We went through the small hall and into the kitchen. 'What's through there?' the officer asked, pointing to a door. I told him that it led to the wine and coal cellars. 'Go down!' he ordered the civilian. We all waited in a tense silence. Then we heard the man's footsteps ascending the stone stairs. 'Nothing there', he reported.

'What's there?' queried the officer, pointing to another door. I told him that opened on to a staircase that led to the bedrooms upstairs. He turned to one of his men, a mechanic as I now realised, and told him to go upstairs and search. The man had a stump of a cigarette hanging from his nether lip. As the man stepped forward, I stepped in front of him.

'I don't allow strangers to smoke in the bedrooms', I said.

The officer said: 'I'll go myself.' I followed him upstairs. In the first room we entered I said to the officer: 'I've never had any experience of this sort of thing, but if I were in charge I'd begin by asking for identity papers', and so saying I took my papers out of my wallet and threw them on the bed. The officer picked them up and looked at them.

'Oh, you're English', he said, speaking in English.

'Surely you'd know that by my accent', I anwered.

He pointed to various doors and asked, in English, whence they led. I told him, but he did not investigate further. We went downstairs; there was an embarrassed silence, then they said goodnight. I took them to the gate and locked it behind them. The guns were rumbling in the distance. I returned to the cottage, and the garden bell tinkled again. There were the same men. I opened up.

'You have a typewriter?' enquired the officer.

'I have two', I replied.

'Can I see them?'

'Certainly.'

We all went into my study in the front of the house. They ignored the typewriters.

'That thing in the corner is a dictaphone', I volunteered.

'What is that?' asked the officer.

I demonstrated the dictaphone. They were all enchanted. They all went out of the room; in the hall the officer and one of the men whispered together.

'Look here', said the officer. 'We are looking for a short-wave transmitter; we think it's located round here; can't you help us?'

Then, like Little Audrey, I laughed and laughed and laughed as the explanation of the raid occurred to me.

Every morning my secretary sat at her desk in my study, the headpiece of the dictaphone clamped to her ears, her fingers on the keyboard of the typewriter. Anyone passing along the road could look over the laurel hedge and see her—transmitting messages on a short-wave transmitter! Incidentally, they did find such a machine in a nearby street, the already mentioned rue Blanche.

Now the French army was astride the river Oise, trying to form a front from Couchy to Péronne, but deserters poured back, mingling with the civilian refugees and reporting that German motor-cyclists and light tanks were circling round the flanks of the French formations. The French newspapers still did not publish the German war communiqués, but I heard them on the B.B.C.; they now sounded like a guide book to northern France. Towns fell like ninepins, without much fighting. Then the Germans announced that General Giraud had been taken prisoner at Wassigny, but the French did not know; he was captured seated inside a tank. Then the Germans captured Sedan, and for the second time in French history this little town sealed the fate of France. That night, for the first time, I heard a terrific artillery bombardment.

In the morning I moved out of my cottage to a less lonely spot, to a small hotel in the Lys forest, about half a mile off the main Amiens-Paris road. I found the forest full of motor lorries piled high with stores; the officers were billeted on the hotel. Soon after I settled in German planes came over. I stood with the air officers whose mess was also in the hotel; we watched the planes in the early evening sky. All of a sudden the planes began dropping bombs; one could see the falling bombs and the burst of sparse anti-aircraft shells. Beaumont-sur-Oise, a few miles away, was being bombed. There was absolutely no danger where we were standing, but the airmen ran into the hotel, shouting over their shoulders for me to follow them. Later I talked to the officers; they were part of the 15th Army Corps, whose headquarters were in Marseilles. They were defeatists to a man.

'It's all up; it's no good going on fighting. Chamberlain is in the hands of the Jews. Paris will be taken; the Germans will take the Channel ports and then advance up the valley of the Seine and take Paris.'

I got talking to a swarthy young corporal with an embryo black beard. He said that in civilian life he ran a garage in Monte Carlo. He said to me: 'You can't help admiring the *cran* (guts) of the Boches. Two days ago when we were in Rheims I heard there was a Boche airman in hospital, with both legs off. I speak a bit of German, so I got permission to have a few minutes with him. He said to me: "I've lost my legs, but Hitler will be in Paris on June 14th".'

The corporal looked at me shrewdly. 'You don't like our officers?' he asserted a query.

'I don't like the tone of their talk', I replied carefully. The corporal shrugged.

'They are all *Action Française* (Royalist-Fascist)', he replied. After dinner that night I took a walk in the forest and met soldiers walking about in the dark shooting with their rifles into the trees. They said they were shooting at parachutists.

Then came the news that Amiens had fallen.

Just before the Germans entered the city some French staff officers were talking to the stationmaster about evacuating the railway employees, when the stationmaster's little boy went to his father and said: '*Your* telephone is ringing.' The station-master waved the boy away, but one of the officers slipped out and went to the office; no phone bell was ringing and he was intrigued. He beckoned to the little boy and whispered: 'Where is your father's telephone?' At that moment the stationmaster looked round, paled, and suddenly ran towards the nearby river Somme, the officers after him. The stationmaster jumped in the river and began swimming. The officers shot at him with their revolvers and hit him. He sank out of sight. The station building was searched and a secret telephone instrument was found.

At that time the Germans were making frequent use of the telephone to spread terror and confusion as they advanced. I had proof of that in my own village, Chantilly.

Late one night the mayor's telephone rang. A voice said it was the Prefect of the Oise Department speaking. Chantilly was to be evacuated immediately by the civilian population. The mayor woke the town crier and sent him on his rounds to wake the population and order them to leave at once. It was then between midnight and one a.m. There was a panic. Those who like myself had a car, loaded up and started out; others set out on foot, dragging children who were crying from fear and fatigue; bed-ridden relatives were lifted on to push-carts and wheel barrows. The following day it was discovered that the call had been put through by a Fifth Columnist.

Then General Gamelin was dismissed and placed under house arrest at Neuilly on the outskirts of Paris. He was suc-ceeded by General Weygand. There came the news of the resignation of Premier Chamberlain; but the French said that had come too late. Up came another exciting crop of rumours: Gamelin had been shot; Roosevelt was going to declare war that very night! Then Reynaud dropped Bonnet from his Government, but he took in Marshal Pétain. I learned from one of my usual informants that on May 15th, late at night, Weygand had tried to telephone Premier Reynaud that the Government should leave Paris, but Reynaud, shut up in his flat with his mistress, according to the book *J'Accuse*, had given orders that he was not to be disturbed, so the message was never delivered.

Now the Paris police were armed with rifles, to prevent German parachutists landing in the capital. I moved again, this time into a small hotel at Neuilly, and once again I went to see Captain Gielgud. I had been interviewed previously by an Intelligence Corps officer who had been flown over from London. First of all I had to listen to the story of a long motor tour he had made before the war in the Atlas Mountains in North Africa. Then he asked me if I spoke German well enough to pass myself off as a German. I said no. Then, could I pass myself off, in Germany, as a Frenchman? I said that was possible. Then, did I think that Italy would enter the war? I said yes, I did. The officer replied: 'That is not our information; a prominent Italian shipbuilder who was with us recently told us that Italy would definitely not enter the war.' That conversation took place exactly two months before Italy did enter the war. Now at the British Military Attaché's office I was told there was 'no news' for me. I walked round the corner and sat on the terrace of the Café Weber in the rue Royale and had a drink. The waiter asked me to pay him when he served me, thus breaking the age-old tradition that in France, indeed all over the Continent, one paid when leaving. The waiter told me that the reason was that when there was an air-raid alarm people went off without paying. I told the waiter, jokingly, that evidently British war-time nerves were stronger than the French. A Frenchman at the next table who overheard me burst into indignant anger. He said to the waiter: 'If he doesn't like it, call a policeman!' I pointed to a sergent de ville, standing on the curb with a rifle slung over his shoulder. 'Why don't you call him?' But I was hustled away to avoid an 'incident'.

Pressure on the British forces was now so great that British planes based on home airfields were crossing the Channel, bombing German columns, and then flying back to re-fuel and load up with new stocks of bombs to start all over again. Air bases in northern France had become untenable, while the usage of French bases further south was uncertain.

One day, at that time, Weygand proposed to go to either Dunkirk or Calais by electric train, but at the last moment General Georges sent a despatch saying the Germans had cut that line of communication. The only contact between Paris and the Channel coast was by plane. Weygand's mission was to meet King Leopold of Belgium, General Gort and General Billotte. At that meeting it was decided that the Belgian Army was to try and hold the line they held on the river Yser, in 1914, facing east; Franco-British divisions were to attack along the Baupaume-Cambrai line, while another French force was to attack on the other side of the open breach in the Allied line, thus the Germans would be attacked on two flanks. But disasters followed swiftly on those decisions; General Billotte met with a motor-car accident and was replaced by General Blanchard, who was almost immediately taken prisoner. Weygand could not fly back to Paris because German planes barred the way. Weygand then left Dunkirk in a destroyer to meet Churchill and Reynaud. I learned secretly that for the past week King Leopold had been bombarding Churchill with messages daily begging him to do something to save the Belgian Army. Then he sent a despairing message to Weygand. Weygand signalled Gort asking him to attack, but, without troubling to inform Weygand of his intention, King Leopold now ordered his Army to lay down their arms. Weygand received a signal from Blanchard's headquarters asking for instructions, 'because the English are embarking at Dunkirk, leaving much material behind'. Weygand signalled: 'Hold Dunkirk bridgehead at all costs.'

On June 1st I drove back to my Chantilly cottage from Neuilly to think things out alone. When I left Paris there was panic. In the morning I sat on the terrace of a small café on the Avenue de Neuilly, watching two streams of traffic, one pouring into the city, the other pouring away from it. The first stream was coming from Normandy; the other flowing into Normandy. The strange part of this nightmare procession was the similarity in the appearance of the two streams of traffic; every car, whether going out or coming in, had one or two mattresses roped to the roof, to serve the double purpose of protection from the bullets of low-flying German planes and to provide sleeping accommodation in case the travellers became stranded. Close inspection did, however, provide one aspect of difference among some of the incoming cars; festooned around the bonnets were crates full of live chickens and ducks.

What should I do? I could not make up my mind.

I garaged the car and took a walk in Chantilly forest. Never in all the years I had lived in France had I known such a wonderful summer. The winter had been hard indeed, when for days the trees in the forest were covered with frozen cobwebs, like fairy woven lace. Now there were still masses of liles of the valley; never had I known such sweet profusion. The springy mossy carpet of the forest was covered with masses of pale blue violets, and bunches of yellow primroses starred the knolls. The hot sunshine shone through a lattice-work of green; birds in their hundreds twittered and sang. And all the time I heard the rumble of distant gunfire. It seemed obscene that there should be such an abundance of the beauties of Nature on the edge of a bloody battlefield.

I took my favourite walk, down by a quarry and then along a hidden path to a place in the middle of the forest where amidst a belt of massive oaks there were fifty to sixty tall and graceful pines. The tornado that had swept across France in the previous March had brought down about half of the pines. I sat on the log of one of them and tried to think.

What should I do? Could France be saved? Could there be another Miracle of the Marne?

Should I try to get to England and chance my luck there?—but how to abandon a land where I had lived and loved and worked and played all my adult years?

I began to think of hiding. I knew the forest well and the innumerable hide-outs, but common sense told me that when the Germans came, as I was sure they would, it would be difficult to avoid a Frenchman handing me over. British stock in France was touching an all-time low. Then I thought of what I had seen driving down from Paris.

There were French Army stragglers on the road, soldiers who had thrown away their rifles. Many of them wore red armbands and gave the clenched fist Communist salute as I drove past them. At Pierrefitte, where the Beauvais road joins the Amiens road to Paris, opposite the petrol pumps, they had placed a light tank in the middle of the forked road and were camouflaging it with boughs torn from nearby trees. Just one tank to defend Paris against a German attack coming from the north! Further along the road towards Chantilly, two burnt-out lorries had been turned on their sides to form a sort of barricade, but along the whole of the twenty-five mile drive I had seen only six 1918 model *mitrailleuses* in the ditches along the roadside. Here and there a Moroccan soldier was slowly helping to build a tank trap. I returned to my cottage, my mind still in a turmoil.

That night all was black and still and the skies covered with millions of twinkling stars. A nightingale was singing in the trees opposite and a tobacco plant beneath my dining-room window was a heavenly scent. After the false evacuation alarm about half the population had returned to Chantilly. I went to the Hotel Condé bar that night. Nothing had changed. The white-coated barman Georges was still playing cards with Charlie Elliot the jockey and two Frenchmen; Bill Sweeper, a retired trainer near on eighty, was about to take his habitual evening walk with his habitual companion, Matt MacGee, the once-famous American jockey. And the Germans were but twenty-five miles away. Then suddenly, my mind was made up; I went back to my cottage with the decision that I would not abandon France.

Chapter III

FIRST OF ALL I returned once again to Paris, to see what was going on there. I went to the British Consulate because I wanted to know their intentions with regard to British citizens. I found they had absolutely none, apart from advising British subjects who had no reason for remaining in Paris, to leave. This was very sound advice for the many British tourists who were still in Paris, but it was of very little use to the thousands of British residents in Paris and in the Paris area. I made enquiries among the members of the staff whom I knew, and was told to my very great surprise that no arrangements had been made for the eventual evacuation of British subjects. All that the Consulate could tell enquirers was that it 'believed' that there was some sort of service functioning from St Nazaire. I was glad to hear that so far as the Consulate itself was concerned it had no intention of leaving Paris, but I should perhaps say here and now that in less than a week the Consul and his entire staff vanished without giving any notice of departure; consequently many thousands of British subjects whose names, addresses and telephone numbers had been registered with the Consulate, in the traditional manner, were absolutely stranded.

From the Consulate I walked the few yards to Captain Gielgud's office. He asked me if I intended leaving. I told him I had no intention of going, not till I had orders from his office. He appeared to be glad to hear what I had to say, and told me that I must keep in constant touch with him, which naturally I agreed to do. Then I went to visit two of the three British banks in Paris. At Lloyds Bank and at the Westminster Bank there was much uncertainty. One bank had sent its papers to Bordeaux and the other to Nantes. That day the French Government announced it was not leaving Paris. Out in the streets people were scurrying about like terrified ants. I drove once again along the Avenue de Neuilly, where now I saw municipal watercarts strung out along the thoroughfare at regular intervals, in order to prevent German transport planes landing. But there were practically no anti-aircraft guns and still no more than half a dozen barrage balloons.

Next day I was lunching with an acquaintance at Lemercier's in the rue Marignan, which was one door off the Avenue des Champs Elysées. Georges Carpentier, I remember, was sitting at the next table. While we were lunching, Paris was bombed for the first time in the war. The restaurant was packed, but nobody stirred; the waitresses carried on perfectly calmly. Nobody knew how many people were killed and injured; according to reports, there were hundreds, but some time later I saw an official report which stated that a thousand people were killed. My luncheon companion was a photographic cartoonist, a Dane who at that time was quite famous for his anti-German cartoons; very clever they were, too. We strolled across the Avenue after lunch. The Champs Elysées was deadly still. An air-raid warden fussily told us to take cover. My Danish friend, who spoke French with a strong guttural accent, began to argue; then a crowd gathered, and I had to drag my friend away, because I heard people murmuring: 'Boches' and 'Anglais'. It struck me at the moment how curious it was that 'Boches' and 'Anglais' on French tongues sounded like enemy words, but naturally, everybody's nerves were on edge. That night there was talk of a military coup d'état; I do not think that it would have been unpopular, but in the event, nothing happened.

The next day I was back again in Chantilly because I simply could not tear myself away. I was working peacefully in the garden when I heard the guns. The weather was dull and heavy, so I tried to persuade myself that it was the rumble of distant thunder. But very soon German planes appeared flying towards Paris; the sky was literally thick with them. Here and there was a little machine-gunning; I could hear the bullets pattering, so I went down to my cellar. I came out and resumed work in the garden after a while, but then I heard bombs begin to fall, some way away. Later I heard that the airfield at Le Bourget had been laid flat. Then once again comedy merged with tragedy.

I thought I would go and get my hair cut. I was in the habit of frequenting a small barber's shop on the Place de la Gare, outside Chantilly railway station. I fetched my car and drove up towards the station. I saw two road-menders sheltering under a tree, as men do during a shower of rain. It was just at that moment that a big cloud of black smoke went up in the air, and then another and another; my car rocked, but I really heard no noise. I cut out the engine and got out and lay flat on the ground. There were columns of black smoke continuing to go up, and then explosions; then a silence so acute that it really hurt. Although I was untouched and unharmed in the middle of a circle of ruins, I was absolutely bewildered. I was a few yards away from Primrose Lodge, a large estate; one of the wings was completely demolished; all the windows, hundreds of them, in a large block of flats, where I had previously lived, about fifty yards from where I was, were completely shattered. The racecourse station, which since the war had been a goods yard, behind the block of flats, was utterly destroyed. Then I drove on to the hairdresser's.

All the plate glass and windows on the Place de la Gare were smashed. Then I saw a figure swathed in white, as if he had escaped from a coffin, with one half of his face covered with soap lather, running like one demented, round and round the Place de la Gare. I went into the hairdresser's, where the boss and his assistant were as white as the sheets they put round their customers' necks. I asked if I should come back later for a haircut. A croaking voice said: 'Yes, please. Come back Monday.' It happened to be Thursday. Then I went on to a *bistro* known locally as 'Petit Louis'. There were cellars there, dating back centuries, with subterranean corridors which were said to lead down to the cellars of Chantilly Castle. The *bistro* was crowded. I got into conversation with some Foreign Legion cavalry. They were Spaniards who had been fighting against Franco in Spain. Now they formed part of the

83

French Ninth Army which had broken and run away. While we were having a drink, the sirens sounded, and the Air Force ground staff, which filled the *bistro*, rushed for the cellars. No civilians could get down because of the crowd of soldiers, who got there first. Then the non-commissioned officers came and ordered them out, but they refused to come up. After the raid I got into conversation with one of the non-commissioned officers, a fellow named Maurice, who had not gone down into the shelters. He asked me to drive him to the goods yard to see the damage. He said it was full of locomotives moved down from the junction at Creil. He told me that the engines had only arrived the previous night, so there was no question at all but that Chantilly must have sheltered spies at that moment. While we were driving to the station Maurice told me that one of his friends had crashed the previous night over Senlis because he had fallen asleep. He said the French had insufficient men and machines.

The goods yard was a shambles. Three planes had done the whole damage to Chantilly. All rolling stock was smashed and heaven knows how many locomotives were completely destroyed. Seven men had been killed. The stationmaster asked me to break the news of the death of one of his employees to his wife, who lived next door to the 'Petit Louis', so we drove back there again. Then there was another air raid; Maurice and I watched it together. We distinctly saw two parachutists bale out of a plane and land somewhere in the neighbourhood of Coye. I imagined that the main viaduct which carried the main line to Paris was the target for the German planes. One of the reserve soldiers guarding that viaduct was Georges, the barman of the 'Condé', but I had never known him to be on duty. But so many queer things were happening that it was difficult to keep count of them. One of my neighbours was the famous trainer Jack Cunnington. He was the third generation of racehorse trainers. He had been born in France, so he could count as a Frenchman, and he had obtained some kind of easy-going job in the French Army.

French officers were always coming to his house. His wife was a German from the Saar. On the morning after the heavy air raid I asked if she intended leaving. She laughed. 'No fear', she said.

After the raid I went back to my garden and worked until it was dark; I went to bed at two in the morning, but I could not sleep. There was an unearthly silence, broken only by creaking furniture. It seemed as if the whole stilled world around me was waiting on some tremendous upheaval. I fell asleep, but was awakened by a horde of German planes; a few seconds later I heard such a bombardment that it pounded the earth. Later in the day I learned it was the bombardment of the convoy I had seen in the Lys forest. I went to our local town hall and while I was there there was an air-raid alarm, and I watched the bombardment of Senlis, about six miles away. Senlis was the little city the Germans burned in 1914. That morning in 1940 it went up in flames again. I heard then that the Germans had destroyed Compiègne and Beauvais. When I returned to my cottage and was preparing to leave for Paris, there was another air raid. I had left my car outside the garden gate, and had locked the doors. There was the usual scamper of Flying Corps men to the forest trench shelters. Then I happened to look out of a window, and saw two of the men, with Red Cross armbands, trying to force the doors of my car. I went to the front door and called out: 'What are you doing?' The two men ran away.

Very soon afterwards, when the 'raiders passed' signal had sounded, I was just unlocking the car and was getting ready to leave, when two armed gendarmes showed up, accompanied by the two would-be thieves. The gendarmes said they had come to arrest me as a spy. I have no doubt at all that the two Red Cross men I had seen trying to rob the car believed that I would be able to identify them, so they had stolen a march on me, and denounced me for having false identity plates. Actually the situation was this: inside the car I had M.C. plates for use when I took the car to England. I made the gendarmes get into the car and drive to the town hall, where I was allowed, somewhat doubtfully perhaps, to go free.

When I got to Paris, I heard the news that the Cabinet had been re-shuffled once again. For the first time Colonel de Gaulle had become a member of the Government; he was Under-Secretary for War, and he had been promoted from Colonel to General. Edouard Daladier had been sacked from the Cabinet by Reynaud. Nobody had ever heard of de Gaulle. I made enquiries and found that he was said to be an expert on mechanised warfare, and had written a book on the subject. It was at this time that I heard a great deal more about Laval, who was intriguing to work Reynaud out and become Prime Minister himself. He was telling everyone that England was already defeated and that the Germans would 'soon' be in London. Late that night I learned that at the Foreign Office on the Quai d'Orsay they were burning documents.

That night I stayed in Paris; in the morning I drove back to Chantilly, realising at last that the beginning of the end had arrived. For days I had been driving up and down between Chantilly and Paris, always trying to discover whether there was any hope of the German advance being halted, but although there were fifty-four French divisions between Paris and the Germans, the whole of the French Army was in full retreat. The line Weygand had been holding, and which was supposed to be so strong, had been abandoned. In Chantilly itself I found a resigned officialdom. There was the silence of death. I drove to my cottage, and for the last time I walked in my garden among the flowers and vegetables I had grown. Crimson sweet peas were on a trellis against a wall of green foliage. Then, while I walked and waited, I heard the roll of the drum of the town crier breaking the silence of awe. I knew that in a few moments he would be at his next stand, only a few yards from my garden gate. I went out of the garden to hear what he had to say now. He turned the corner on his bicycle, dismounted, unslung his drum, and sounded a roll. No crowd gathered now; I was the only person standing in the glaring sun to whom he read his message. It was short: Chantilly was to be evacuated before midnight that night, by order of the military authorities. The crier gave another roll on his drum and slung his instruments, crossed over to a tree and urinated, then he mounted his bicycle and rode away. The ensuing silence was pierced by distant gunfire, which rumbled on and on. Was it German; was it French? One knew, of course, but one had to hope. I stood stunned with misery and despair.

In a minute or two my neighbour Jack Cunnington, the racehorse trainer, and an old Englishman named Esling, came out of the forest. Esling was the father of the famous English jockey who used to ride in France. I noticed that both men looked at me very curiously, then they looked at one another. 'What's the matter with you?' I asked.

'If any of them catch you now, it will be a bad look-out for you', Esling said. I thought he was referring to the Germans.

'They won't catch me here', I said. 'I'm going to start for Paris as soon as I have loaded the car.'

'Not the Germans', the old Englishman grinned. 'The French people; they say you are a Nazi agent, and that you use your car as a signal to their airmen. Every time you park it here they come over and bomb this place.'

I could see he was not quite sure himself whether this was true or not. We talked for a minute or two. Jack Cunnington was optimistic; he said the Germans might be in Chantilly for a day or two—'like last time'—'but', he said, 'the British are going to land again and everything will be all right.'

Esling said: 'As long as we keep this side of the Seine, we shall be all right. The Germans will never cross the Seine.' He said he was going to stay on his son's farm in Normandy. Would I drive him to Paris? I asked him to help me load the car. The noise of the guns now grew louder.

We went into the cottage and stripped the beds and carried two mattresses downstairs and fastened them with rope to the roof of the car. I packed some clothes and some books. Esling had already killed his poultry; he had just a small bag and a little white dog; he was ready. I locked up and put the keys of the cottage in my pocket. It had been ordained by the mayor that all houses in Chantilly had to be placed under his protection, and keys were to be given up to him. Esling and I drove to the *mairie* and gave up our keys, and then took to the main road.

There were soldiers everywhere, straggling along, many giving the Communist salute and laughing. At Sarcelles I had to slow down because of a drunken orgy. The villagers were emptying their cellars and were giving the red and white wine to the soldiers, who were gulping it down and weaving backwards and forwards across the road. I was driving a Flying Standard car that had a miniature enamel Union Jack on the bonnet. When the soldiers saw the British flag they made rude noises.

Then from a side road leading from Beaumont-sur-Oise came a soldier-chauffeur-driven car with an officer sitting in the back. He checked his car, alighted, and tried to quieten the men, but they would not listen to him. They hooted at him, joined hands in a circle and danced round him, inviting him to drink. He shrugged his shoulders, returned to his car and drove away.

I had cut out my engine, and now I started it up again and began to edge slowly through the milling crowd, towards Paris. I had not proceeded a dozen yards when a soldier, waving a handkerchief in one hand and a revolver in the other, jumped in front of the car; I thought he was merely another drunk, and I waved him away. Fortunately for me, my windscreen was wide open, so I heard him scream: 'Stop or I fire!'

I stopped, and beckoned him to the side of the car. He was a Battle Policeman, very drunk, but nevertheless a Battle Policeman. That was eighteen miles from Paris on Sunday, June 9th, 1940.

He told me I could not proceed to Paris, but I could take the side road to Beaumont-sur-Oise. I backed the car among the drunken, cursing soldiers, and turned off to the right. I had to drive against a stream of army lorries full of soldiers who had been bombed by diving Stukas at Creil; time and time again Esling and I had to stop the car, alight and crawl into ditches as German planes swooped and hedge-hopped, machine-gunning. I reached the Beaumont main road and, dodging shell craters, drove on towards Paris while thick columns of black smoke were shooting up all around us as the bombs dropped, but we came through unscathed, although death was at my heels.

At Pierrefitte petrol pumps, where we joined the Amiens-Paris main road again, we were stopped by two gendarmes and asked to show our passes. I asked Esling to get out and see whether the mattresses were all right. After we were rolling again Esling suddenly said: 'Where's my dog?' The dog must have jumped out after his master. We could not go back. That night Esling took train from Paris to Normandy, despite all my efforts to dissuade him. He fell into the hands of the Germans and I never heard of him again.

Back in Paris my useful friends told me of the events of the previous three days. While the German 5th and 7th Panzer divisions were driving through the Normandy apple orchards, Reynaud was trying to bribe Mussolini to stay out of the war. But Reynaud had told my friend Léon Bassée of the Havas Agency: 'It's no good. Ciano told François Poncet (the French Ambassador at Rome): "Even if you offered us the whole of Tunisia, that wouldn't be any use. Italy is going to war."' Bassée also informed me that although Reynaud had broadcast over the wireless that the Government was going to remain, secret preparations had been made for leaving Paris. The Government would travel in two convoys; Reynaud and a few other members of the Cabinet were to travel in the second convoy. Yves Delbos, whom I used to meet at Geneviève Tabouis', was down to go with the first convoy, but he opposed the whole scheme.

That night I walked down to the Porte Maillot. A few lorries full of troops passed; they seemed in fine fettle and were screaming: '*On les aura!*', the wary cry of the victorious *poilus* at Verdun, but now there were no echoing cries of encouragement from the pavements of Paris. Everyone believed what Ferdonnet had broadcast from Stuttgart; Hitler said the Germans will enter Paris on June 14th. He was correct, as usual.

Chapter IV

WHILE I WAS still waiting on the order of my going, now, June 10th, I was awakened shortly before dawn by the sound of a dull explosion; my room in the Neuilly hotel, where I had taken refuge, shook. At eight o'clock I went out to get some milk; there was no milk; milk for this section of the city came from Mantes; the explosion I had heard was Mantes Bridge blowing up. The Germans had attacked at Vernon and cut the French Tenth Army in half; one British division and two French divisions had been surrounded, and most of them were prisoners, but the Germans now had more prisoners than they could cope with, so they disarmed them and turned them loose, and so added to the general confusion. Then I heard that the Germans were in Chantilly.

General de Gaulle had been to London to try and persuade Churchill to let France have a strong R.A.F. force, and to discuss the return of part of the B.E.F. to France, in order to establish a bridgehead in Brittany. De Gaulle reported to Reynaud the failure of his mission. That evening a French journalist and I had dinner on the terrace of a small Neuilly restaurant. There was a long wait between courses; then the waitress came out crying.

'Italy has declared war on us', she said. 'I just heard it on the wireless; this is the end.'

My friend and I drove down to the Foreign Office on the Quai d'Orsay; the night air was acrid with the smell of burning paper. We drove down town; there was even more refugee traffic than usual. We went back to the Foreign Office, where we learned that the Government had to leave before midnight; it was going to Tours. I heard Reynaud on the wireless; he said he was going to the armies, but as soon as he finished his broadcast he left Paris with his mistress. President Lebrun and the whole Government left together, but they were held up near Chartres by a mass of refugees. In the midst of the confusion German planes appeared. It was pitch dark and the Germans did not see the convoy; no bombs were dropped; if they had been, the whole Government would have been wiped out that night.

Later, I heard the full story; the fleeing Government arrived on the banks of the Loire river, looking like a caravan of gypsies. Everywhere there was confusion. Some Ministries were at Tours; other at Langeais, Azay-le-Rideau and Ligueil, but the local telephone exchanges had not been advised, so there were no telephonic communications between the various Ministries. The President was at Cangey, Georges Mandel had his office in the Tours Préfecture. Reynaud was missing, so Camille Chautemps, the Deputy Premier, presided at the first meeting of the Cabinet.

Here I was, like a rabbit in a partially disused rabbit warren; Paris was that warren, and there I was scuttling about, not wanting to break my promise to Colonel Gielgud, but wondering what I could do with all these news stories breaking around me; my journalistic instincts were strong; yet I knew that unless I moved out of Paris, and quickly, I would be trapped like any other rabbit. Dart into a hole; but which?

I had an English friend named Hardman Lucas, who had family connections in a hamlet called St Fortunat, in the Ardèche Department. I arranged to go into hiding there with him, his wife and daughter; we were to meet at the Porte d'Italie at six p.m. on June 11th, and I was to follow them in my car. When I started out I knew that the railway stations were not selling any more tickets; bicycles were at a premium; petrol was hard to come by; anything that rolled on wheels, including hearses, was being sought by the thousands who wanted to escape from Paris. There was great excitement. There was a mist, but it was not a heat mist; it was something that got into one's eyes and nostrils; it stayed on one's face; my windscreen and my hands were covered with this thing; it turned into black smudges and blotted out the sun. I went into a *bistro* and had a coffee. People were saying this thing was sent by God to protect Paris from German airmen; they said that in some parishes of Paris priests were parading statues of the patron saint of Paris, Sainte Geneviève. Others sniffed the mist and said it smelt of burnt wood; it was the smoke of burning cities. And I, I could smell nothing. To me it was just the funeral pall of Paris. I was terribly unhappy; tears were running down my cheeks. I spoke to no one. I looked for the Hardman Lucases and could not see them. I waited and waited and then edged my car into the stream of traffic passing through the Porte d'Italie. And that was the last time I saw Paris for five and a half years. I, like thousands of French people, was running away, but whence I did not know.

I headed first for Fontainbleau, but soldiers were making motorists by-pass Fontainbleau; the Paris smog was here, too. Now one ran into a stream of oncoming motor traffic; hundreds and hundreds of cars with B.A. number plates, the matriculation letters of the Basses Alpes, the Alpes Maritime department; in other words, French people fleeing from the invading Italians, while we were fleeing in the opposite direction from the invading Germans. Every now and again the flow of traffic was halted while a car was dragged out of the stream: a broken axle or a snapped chain. All that day I drove on and on, but isolated from the free world.

I reached Nevers in the evening. It was completely dark. I had been driving continuously for twelve hours. My petrol tank was empty and I was exhausted, but no inn had any room for me. Nevers was packed out with refugees. Then I remembered the name of a French family with English connections: a Frenchman who had married an English girl. I traced them and was given a welcome, food and a bed. All through the night German planes were over Nevers and a bomb dropped in the garden of a convent behind the house where I stayed. The next morning early I was on my way again.

It was June 12th, 1940. I did not know it then, but I knew later that the Reynaud Government at Tours was divided in purpose; some Ministers favoured orders stopping the evacuation of refugees to free the roads for the movement of troops, but no decision was taken. Rheims fell; the French Seventh Army had fallen back from Senlis almost to the gates of Paris, while the Germans crossed the Seine at Vernon. But in Tours confusion increased.

From various sources I was able to piece together this amazing story: Paul Reynaud arrived late that June afternoon and called a meeting of the Cabinet under the chairmanship of President Lebrun. It was called at the Château de Cangey. Although the meeting was scheduled for four p.m., no Ministers arrived, because there had been a mix-up. Cangey is close to Candé, where the Duke of Windsor married Mrs Wallis Simpson; that name was a familiar one, so it was to the Château de Candé, instead of the Château de Cangey, that the French Ministers went. Finally, everything was straightened out, and the Cabinet met at the Château de Cangey between seven-thirty and eight p.m. that evening; but four very precious hours had been lost, while the Germans were poised for the fall of Paris. At Reynaud's behest, Weygand was present at this Cabinet meeting. He was asked to make a statement. He defended himself by attacking others, chiefly Gort; Weygand said Gort had refused to carry out his orders. Weygand further said: 'I was given an impossible job; I fought a second battle to save the honour of France.' Weygand was then questioned. He said that Paris could not be defended. Then there were more questions and Weygand finally said: 'I'll continue to fight if the Government orders me to do so, but in my opinion the war is lost, definitely lost. I don't want to see France handed over to the Communists.' Pétain chimed in: 'Better Hitler than Communism.' Weygand continued: 'It's my job now to keep order.'

The Cabinet then discussed the problem; whether to sue for an Armistice or to continue resistance? There followed a remarkable scene. During the discussion night had fallen. One of the Paris Foreign Office ushers, the men in the black coats, knee-breeches and silver chains round their necks, came in to turn on the lights. He had accompanied the Minister from Paris. The political discussions stopped while the usher fumbled for the switches; naturally, he was not familiar with the layout of the Castle rooms, but everybody's nerves were on edge; tension grew; the usher found one switch but seemingly he could not find any others. Suddenly the last President of the Third French Republic, Albert Lebrun, could stand it no longer.

'Get out!' he screamed at the trembling usher. Then in semi-obscurity, Jean Prouvost, proprietor of the Parisian evening newspaper *Paris-Soir*, the new Minister of Information, suggested an Armistice. He sneered at the idea of transferring the French Government abroad and was equally caustic about the suggestion of maintaining an Anglo-French bridgehead in Brittany. Yves Delbos pleaded that France must never abandon Britain. Reynaud said he favoured the bridgehead, but he would prefer not making a decision until he had conferred with Churchill; therefore he had arranged to meet Churchill at Nantes at five the following day. Camille Chautemps suggested that Churchill should personally attend a meeting of the French Cabinet in order to obtain a first-hand account of the desperate situation of France. Chautemps was backed up by the majority of the Cabinet. Reynaud said he would telephone Churchill at once, asking him to get to Tours as quickly as possible.

On the night of June 12th I reached Tournan. It was pouring with rain; the flashes of lightning and the grumble of thunder were just like the flashes and the thunder of the German guns. In the little hotel salon a number of very indignant Paris schoolmistresses sat round the radio; they had just heard an announcer tell them, and other refugee teachers, that they should return to their jobs forthwith.

'But', they cried in unison, 'the Government has gone; why shouldn't we go too?'

All the time people hung round radios, waiting for the official bulletins which became more sparse and more and more confused. Each bulletin was preceded by a cracked gramophone record that played the opening bars of the 'Marseillaise', *'Aux armes, citoyens!'*, over and over and over again until one was ready to scream with pent-up frustration. Of what use calling the citizens to arms when the Government and the army and the citizens were running for their lives?

Later I learned more of the secret history of those amazing days. On June 13th, Churchill, Halifax and Lord Beaverbrook flew to Tours and went to the Grand Hotel. Just a year previously Lord Beaverbrook's newspapers had told their readers there would be no war; now he was called to the deathbed of France. Churchill went to the Tours Préfecture accompanied by Major-General Spears, a man more Francophile than the French themselves. One could not imagine a worse adviser on French affairs at that moment than the man Spears.

Churchill must have been amazed when for the first time he heard this question: 'What will England do if France makes a separate peace?' Churchill replied bravely to the effect: 'We won't heap recriminations on the head of an unfortunate partner. If we win, we will make an unconditional promise to raise France from ruin.' Churchill then walked out of the room and conferred in an adjoining room with Halifax and Beaverbrook. While they talked, Reynaud conferred with the Speakers of the French Senate and Chamber of Deputies. Both men,

Jeanneney and Herriot, became angry when Reynaud told them the Government was discussing an Armistice. The argument was interrupted when Reynaud was called to the telephone. It was Roger Langeron, the Paris Prefect of Police, telephoning to say the Germans were now at the gates of Paris. Herriot broke down and wept, which he was in the habit of doing in moments of crisis, and then talked to waiting reporters and told them the bad news. Churchill returned and conferred with Reynaud and Georges Mandel. But at the Château de Cangey members of the Cabinet were awaiting the expected arrival of Reynaud and Churchill. After a wait of nearly two hours, Reynaud's car was seen approaching, but it was noticed that he was alone. Behind him was another car; Mandel also rode alone.

'Where's Churchill?' Chautemps asked Reynaud.

'He's gone back to England', answered Reynaud.

The Cabinet began its delayed meeting. Mandel was astonished when Reynaud told his colleagues that he had informed Churchill that France, far from seeking an armistice, would continue the war. Pétain said he favoured surrender. Then there was a discussion that showed that at that moment the Cabinet was sharply divided: half favoured continuing the war, the other half favoured an armistice. The discussion continued until Reynaud proposed that he should make a last appeal to Roosevelt to declare that the United States would be morally and materially on the side of France. This was finally agreed, but as the meeting was breaking up there came another telephoned message from Paris to say the Germans were entering the capital.

That night, June 13th, at eleven-thirty, I heard Reynaud on the radio telling the waiting world that France was going to fight on! It seemed that just before he went on the air the Premier had won both Pétain and Weygand over to the opinion that whatever happened the French Fleet and what was left of the Air Force must not be allowed to fall into the hands of the Germans and used against Britain.

The next morning at dawn, I drove to St Fortunat via Valance, crossing the bridge over the swift-flowing Rhône. I found the bridge defended by one shabby soldier and a few strands of rusty wire. I drove into the department of the Ardèche, the peach-growing country of France; through it runs the river Eyneux, over a stony bed, to fall into the Rhône. Millions of peach trees cover the valley; the high slate-grey hills that rear so forbiddingly both sides of the river are dotted with tiny hamlets; lost in the hills are numerous villages, as remote as can be. It seemed an excellent hide-away until I knew what to do. Twenty-four of us had been recruited in Paris by the British Military Attaché's office, to form a certain British service. We had all guaranteed that we would not leave Paris without informing the Military Attaché, but in the event, the British Embassy staff and the Consular staff, and the Attachés, of course, all packed up and went without informing anybody, and thus stranded thousands of their compatriots, including the twenty-four who had volunteered and had agreed to risk their liberties and even their lives. And that was why I found myself forlorn in St Fortunat.

Now Ferdonnet from Stuttgart announced that the Germans and Italians 'will join hands in the middle of France'. The intended place was Chambéry, but there was a battle never reported; it caused the Axis staff plans to be changed.

I was not far from Valence, where the French General Olry had his headquarters in the Riding School. I picked up the threads of the story after the battle ended.

The Germans planned to cross the Isère river and, as I wrote, link up with the Italians at Chambéry. But Olry's Army of the Alps had been constantly depleted. When Italy entered the war the only troops he had to hold the line from Switzerland to the Mediterranean consisted of six divisions. His 'reserves' consisted of one Senegalese regiment. Half an hour after Italy declared war, Olry blew up the St Louis bridge, which linked France to Italy at Mentone; then he destroyed every railway tunnel and every little wooden bridge that crossed a mountain stream. The Italians did nothing, doubtless hoping and believing that the Germans advancing from the north would quickly finish off Olry's Army. But on June 16th the Italians did faint-heartedly attack and were repulsed; their patrols were driven back. Then after a pause, the Italians attacked again and in greater force. Now Olry had to fight on two fronts, because the Germans attacked his left flank along the Isère. North of Nice a mere handful of the French Chausseurs Alpin, known as the 'Blue Devils', bluffed the Italians. The French were holding a small concrete fort, but instead of the usual broiling Riviera June sun, there now poured torrential rain, while the lightning flashed and the thunder roared. Then a fog came up. The 'Blue Devils' took advantage of the strange atmospheric conditions by making frequent sorties and taking prisoners, making the Italians think they were up against a large force. But they took so many prisoners that the French did not know what to do. The French commanding officer said to his men: 'All right, keep the Macaronis out of the rain, we'll fight outside.' But one of the prisoners understood French and he overheard and called out: 'No, you come inside with us; we'll crowd together a bit more.'

But further north the fight was grimmer; Olry had a very mixed force defending his left flank there. There were a few sailors with some naval guns; a few sappers; a few thousand infantrymen, some old planes and a small group of tanks. But it was the sappers who turned the trick.

Until the rains came the bed of the river Isère was as dry as it always is in the summertime. Olry's men knew every goat path in the mountains. They had dragged the naval guns across the river bed, up the mountains, and mounted them on the natural artillery emplacements around La Grande Chartreuse. When the German light motorised forces debouched through the valleys they were blown to pieces by the heavy French naval guns perched hundreds of feet up in the mountains. The German High Command contacted Rome. At five thirty-five in the afternoon of June 22nd, Rome wirelessed this message, picked up at Olry's headquarters, to the Italian Alpine Army: 'At all costs you must push ahead and step up your infiltrations, and if necessary throw the Royal Regiment into the attack; I repeat: advance at all costs, without counting sacrifices.'

Although this message was sent only four days before the 'cease fire' order, the Italians did attack and lost twelve hundred prisoners. I have no figures relating to the number of killed and wounded. The French casualties against the Italians from first to last numbered seven hundred.

Now up north the Germans increased their pressure, but Olry had worked out a plan. Hidden in the mountain fastness French-built dams held back millions of tons of snow water from the Alpine rivers and streams. Olry's sappers blew up those dams and released those millions of tons of water. Now the Germans were immobilised by France's liquid ally which held them down on the wrong side of the river Isère, where they were when the 'cease fire' sounded, and so they were not able to link up with their Italian allies, according to plan.

But while those heroic deeds were happening on one side of France, on the other side matters were going from bad to worse. The French Government, as I learned later, moved from Tours to Bordeaux, where Laval and his friend Marquet, a former local Socialist mayor, a dentist now turned Fascist, were in control. President Lebrun, Herriot, Jeanneney, Mandel and Delbos and a few others had arranged to leave Bordeaux for Perpignan and from there to go to a Mediterranean port to take ship to Africa to set up a new Government, but Pétain and Laval bullied the now nerve-racked Lebrun and made him change his mind. Weygand was also in Bordeaux, where he told the Cabinet it must sue for an armistice. Chautemps now had considerable support for his plan to ask Germany for terms for an armistice and eventual peace. Reynaud was waiting for Roosevelt's reply to his message. Only Mandel held out for an uncompromising decision to fight on. Then came

Roosevelt's reply, which was by no means the reply for which Reynaud hoped. Pétain threatened to resign unless the Government asked for an armistice. Then Reynaud disclosed a message he had received from the British Ambassador, Sir Ronald Campbell: the British Cabinet could not implement the promise Churchill had made at Tours.

That night at nine p.m. the Reynaud Cabinet resigned. It was time to draw the curtains.

Chapter V

THE REAL STORY of the surrender of Paris has never been told in any detail; the complete picture came into my hands while I was still hidden in France. The surrender of the French capital was arranged by Mr William Bullitt, the American Ambassador at Paris. It took place near to where I had been living, in a little village called Ecouen. Paris was surrendered in an old house opposite the stone by the roadside which marked the spot where von Kluck's Uhlans were stopped in 1914, when Paris was saved. I was particularly interested in the story because the old house where the surrender took place was one that I had some years previously tried to buy, but I was not allowed to buy it because I was a foreigner; the French War Office had control of the land at the back of the house; there were several places of this kind where they had the right to erect artillery emplacements in case of necessity.

Actually, the last battle for Paris was fought out in a small circle around my Chantilly cottage. The Germans were held up in the Oise valley; they could not drive the French out of the marshy swamps of the Nonette. The bridge over the Oise was under the fire of French artillery; Pont Sainte Maxence was being hammered by French planes, and a

German divisional staff in Chantilly forest had to leave in a great hurry because they were too exposed to French fire. The French fell back on Paris on the morning of June 13th. That was a Thursday. Behind them was a thick column of black smoke; that was when they were burning the petrol pumps at St Denis. The French did put up a fight when they had their backs to Paris. While a French platoon was fighting, two grey German cars came along. Standing on the running-board of the first car was a trumpeter. He sounded the French 'cease fire' call. That was at six-thirty in the evening. The fighting platoon had had no instructions, so the men fired on the German cars. The German officer shouted out something, but the French did not understand what he was saying. Then the second car turned round and drove off towards Chantilly at top speed. The driver of the first car turned into a field and tried to take shelter behind a wall. Then the French guns began to shell the road, but at this moment a strong German force came up and picked up the first car, which contained three German officers; they had come to demand the surrender of Paris, which had that very morning been declared an 'open city'.

Fighting then stopped immediately. The German officers remained all night in Ecouen, and the next morning the village filled up with German troops. The three officers, a major, a captain and a lieutenant, waited the arrival of the envoys from General Héring, the Governor of Paris. Although it was a June morning, the weather was dark and stormy. The Germans sent out for candles, and had them stuck in bottles; they lit the candles and put them around the salon. Then a French staff officer and a German-speaking lieutenant arrived at the house. The German major read out the conditions, paragraph by paragraph, and after he had read each one, it was translated. When that was over, the French staff officer asked what precisely was meant by the word 'Paris'.

'The city and the suburbs', said the German.

'No', said the Frenchman. 'The city only.'

'If Paris does not surrender', said the German, 'at nine o'clock this morning German planes will darken further the Paris skies and the city will be reduced to dust and ashes by German artillery.'

Eventually, the German major said that he would ask further instructions; if he was not back in an hour, 'that would have but one meaning: the utter destruction of Paris'.

The four officers, two German and two French, sat in silence in the salon, smoking. The only sound was the regular tread of the sentry on the stone pavement outside the house. Forty-five minutes later, the major was back. At seven-thirty a.m. the papers were signed, handing over Paris, suburbs and all. And that is how Paris was surrendered by candlelight.

But the proceedings were farcical really, because already at dawn on the 14th, as I learned from refugees, early risers in Paris saw Germans on the Place de la Concorde, and at seven-thirty a.m. two columns of light tanks entered Paris, one by the Porte de la Chapelle, and the other by the Porte de Saint Cloud. So Hitler kept his word; he had always said he would be in Paris on June 14th.

Then a traveller brought me news from Bordeaux, which was full of rumours. It was said that both Reynaud and Churchill had committed suicide. It was also rumoured that Mandel had been arrested and shot. He was not shot, but he had been arrested. He was lunching at the *Chapon Fin*, Bordeaux's best restaurant, with his lady friend from the Comédie Française, when a lieutenant of gendarmerie walked into the restaurant and asked Mandel to step outside. He was held for an hour and then released. That night Pétain went on the air. I heard his shaky old voice announce that France must stop fighting. The next day it became known that Baudoin was trying to prevent the Belgian Ministers from going to England. President Lebrun was still pleading that he might be allowed to go to North Africa, while both the British and the American Ambassadors were asking Baudoin to give an assurance that the French Fleet would not be handed over to the Germans.

Pétain had been told by the Germans to send a delegation to sue for armistice terms, but he was also told he would have to telegraph to Mussolini to know the Italian terms. My informant said Baudoin himself seemed highly nervous. He asked the Spanish Ambassador to beg Hitler to stop the Germans marching on Bordeaux. On this day, said my informant, there was a secret meeting of French Deputies in a schoolhouse in the rue Anatole France, where they tried to work out a *coup d'état* to stop the rot that had set in, but close by, in the Town Hall, sat Laval and Marquet, who had their own secret agents keeping them informed of everything that was happening in the schoolhouse. Under Laval's pressure, Pétain issued an order that any politician who decided to go to North Africa must first of all sign away his parliamentary rights. Then Churchill sent Lord Lloyd and Mr A. V. Alexander to Bordeaux to beg Pétain not to hand over the French Fleet to the Germans.

In St Fortunat I was still wondering what I should do. I heard once again from Bordeaux, when I was told that the city was packed with refugees. Lord Lloyd, Sir Ronald Campbell and Jean Provoust were all at the Hotel Montré, where they had their nights' sleep broken every night by the air-raid alarms. During one air-raid, thirty people were killed and a hundred had to go to hospital. During the air-raid Lord Lloyd and Jean Provoust sat on the stairs and talked, but Campbell kept apart because he and Provoust were not on speaking terms since Provoust told Campbell: 'You can't win a war with a million and a half unemployed.' Then, the following day, Provoust told Lord Lloyd that Churchill was wrong in backing Mandel.

I was staying in a small hotel in St Fortunat. A man arrived from Dijon, in a motor-car, with his wife and a son and daughter. He was a cousin of the proprietor of the hotel. The Dijon gentleman insisted on taking me up to his bedroom, where from under his bed he drew boxes full of English sovereigns and gold *louis* and packets of American dollar notes. No doubt just a good little patriotic Frenchman.

I heard from Bordeaux again, that President Lebrun was still talking about going to Port Vendres, and from there embarking in a destroyer for Algiers. In the middle of this particular afternoon it was announced in Bordeaux that the *Massilia*, an old 15,000-tonner, was waiting at the mouth of the Gironde. The captain was under the impression that it was to be an official journey to North Africa. The vessel had been chartered by Herriot and Daladier, Mandel, Delbos, and a number of others who were ready to leave; it was clearly understood that Herriot and Jeanneney would be leaving, too, and that a part of Pétain's Government would follow. Then Laval came on the scene. He sent Marquet and some others to Pétain to tell him that no member of his Government should be allowed to leave. Pétain immediately issued this order, at five p.m. At the same time the old Marshal sent a personal telegram to Hitler asking him to stop the German troops from entering Bordeaux before June 30th. On Pétain's orders, Jeanneney, who was then in Toulouse, was held up by the police and forced to return to Bordeaux. I have always understood that Herriot's luggage was actually in the *Massilia's* hold when she sailed, but Herriot stayed behind; whether it was of his own free will or not I never knew.

When the crew of the *Massilia* learned what had happened, they refused to sail, but after Monsieur Campinchi, who was Minister of Marine, made a speech, the ship weighed anchor.

Now in Bordeaux, so I was told, Laval was working hard on Lebrun. He went to see the President and took with him Bonnet, Marquet, Gaston de Bérgery and Pietri. Laval said that in the name of the delegation he forbade the President of the Republic to go to North Africa to carry on the fight. Lebrun could go as a private citizen, but not as President. The text of the actual statement was: 'If you leave France, you'll never set foot there again. Go, if you want. But you don't go as President. You must resign. Give us your resignation!' They waited a few moments, then they turned their backs on Lebrun and walked out of the room. Later that day, Pétain called on Lebrun; no doubt he came from Laval, to put into official wording the threats that had been uttered earlier.

Then General Huntziger telephoned the German armistice terms to Weygand, and about the same time Hitler answered Pétain's appeal not to take Bordeaux yet awhile. Hitler sent his reply from Compiègne, where Germany had received the armistice terms from the victorious allies in November, 1918. The French were not told the armistice terms until some time later. But Baudoin told Ambassador Campbell that if Hitler had insisted on the Fleet being handed over, France would not have accepted the armistice terms.

It became known that the Government had until nine a.m. on June 22nd to accept or reject the armistice conditions. The Cabinet met at one a.m. and sat until three a.m. Lebrun favoured rejection, and so did a part of the Cabinet, but Pétain, no doubt wanting to hear what Laval had to say, adjourned the meeting until eight. After leaving the meeting, Baudoin met Campbell, who asked to be informed of the situation. Baudoin replied sarcastically: 'If you like to ask your Government to request the German Government to extend the brief period accorded to us to consider the terms, I shall be delighted.' Then at the adjourned meeting the Government accepted the armistice conditions, but although they were broadcast by the B.B.C., nothing was said over the French wireless, which by order of the Germans was now closed down at nine p.m. every night. Ambassador Campbell called on Baudoin to say he was leaving for England. Baudoin wanted to know if he was going of his own accord, or whether London had recalled him.

June 23rd, both Lyons and Vichy, which had been occupied by the Germans, were evacuated by them, but when the Germans left Lyons, they carried off fifteen thousand of the French garrison with them. I saw at this time a Grenoble newspaper, which was the only French newspaper I was seeing, which said that every day a German military band was playing

D*

on the Place Bellecour, and that women gathered round and applauded. The newspaper added: '*Elles sont des femmes de mauvaise vie*', suggesting that they were harlots out to get custom. I could not help wondering whether that was actually the case. There appeared to be no antipathy whatsoever towards the Germans. On all sides the French were saying that the British had let them down.

A little later I heard what had happened during the voyage of the *Massilia* to Morocco. Daladier and Mandel listened on the ship's wireless to the speeches of Churchill and de Gaulle; immediately they asked the captain to change the course of his ship and make for England. He refused. They tried to bribe him, but he would not listen. He agreed, however, to go to a Moroccan port instead of to Algiers. But Fate still had other misfortunes in store for the Frenchmen on board. When the *Massilia* arrived at Casablanca, there was an order saying that neither Daladier nor Mandel was to be allowed to land. Laval had made up his mind to hand them over to the Germans. Mandel, however, slipped past the guards, got ashore, and cabled Churchill asking that a plane be sent to fetch him. Two days later a plane arrived; in it were Lord Gort and Sir Duff Cooper. I think that was a very grave mistake; anyhow, their mission failed, and on June 25th it was all over, and the curtain was rung down on the Third Republic. Marshal Pétain decreed a day of national mourning.

BOOK THREE

Chapter I

A LITTLE BEFORE the end of June, 1940, there was already a shortage of food in St Fortunat, the hamlet where I was staying. There was sufficient bread, perhaps, and just about enough meat, but practically no vegetables, and all tinned foods had vanished. There was a lack of wine and oil and coffee and tea and tobacco and matches. I drove up to the mountains twice, to Privas, the county town of the Ardèche, to see what I could do about getting away. The Valence bridge that I have mentioned previously had been blown up, so there was no way of reaching the left bank of the Rhône, except by taking a chance at being shot at and crossing the railway bridge at a place called La Voulte; the single-track line from La Voulte to St Fortunat had ceased working, so to reach La Voulte meant obtaining a seat in the precarious bus that only ran three times a week; alternatively, walking ten miles in either direction.

My trips to Privas were of no avail, but I did obtain a visa which entitled me to go to Spain via Marseilles; that visa would only be of any use if I could find a ship in Marseilles. Learning this, I returned in despair to St Fortunat and wondered what I should do now. Everywhere there was complete defeatism. All that the local people cared about was selling their peaches; for them the war had no meaning at all. France was defeated, and that was that. When the British Fleet bombarded the French Fleet at Mers-el-Kebir there was a tremendous uproar and I had a very difficult time keeping myself from being attacked. It was impossible for me to try and justify that attack, because in my heart of hearts I did not think it could be justified. I thought, and I still think, that the attack was a very unwise move on the part of Churchill. The French Fleet was loyal and I believed and still believe that if the officers had been ordered to hand over their ships to the Germans, they would have done just what the Germans did at Scapa Flow, sunk their ships. But, nevertheless, things were extremely difficult, and I had no idea how I was going to make my way out of France. I obtained a note from the butcher-mayor of St Fortunat to the head of the gendarmerie at La Voulte to ask for a permit to get sufficient petrol to get me to Marseilles again. I obtained it, and had a most uncomfortable journey, because everywhere I had to listen to attacks on Britain. In Marseilles I was fortunate in finding the American Consul-General, Mr John Hurley. When I asked what had happened to the British people in Marseilles, he told me that they had disappeared; there were just a few, stranded, he said.

Mr Hurley had no funds to help the British, but he had helped some of them out of his own pocket. He told me he had cabled Washington and the London Foreign Office but there had been no reply. I found a small hotel called the Hotel de la Préfecture, not far from the Consul's office. I enquired about a garage for my car, and was directed to one where the proprietor told me he had just been mobilised, and that he knew that the British had taken Corsica, so that if I wanted to get away I had better make for Corsica. Then he told me about several bombardments of which I had never heard. Of course, I knew the reputation of the people of Marseilles for the telling of tall stories, and the stories I had just heard turned out to be typical of Marseilles. I went all over the city trying to find a ship, but there was no possibility. One night I was standing at the corner of a street giving on to the Canebière, when I saw a man in a strange uniform; it was neither French nor British, and I thought it might be German. I edged up closely and saw that the man was wearing the uniform of the American Ambulance. I got into conversation with the fellow, who told me his name was Charlie Fawcett. I told him casually that I had in the past written a great deal about an explorer of that name who had disappeared up the river Amazon. 'That's my uncle', said the American ambulance man simply.

With little hope in my heart I drove back to St Fortunat. Paul Reynaud and Georges Mandel, I learned, were now jailed in Chazeron Castle. General Gamelin, Léon Blum and Edouard Daladier had been taken to a prison at Bourrasol. I learned also that Reynaud spent his time doing physical jerks, while Mandel refused to be treated with anything but the respect he said was due an ex-Minister. He told one of his warders this: 'We shall go from defeat to disaster, and then on to final victory.'

Mandel refused to eat the prison fare; his actress friend was staying at Chatelguyon; she was allowed to visit Mandel once a week, but every day she sent him food which was brought to him by a black servant in a gazogene-driven motor-car.

I tried in vain to explain to the French people around me that the Germans were taking their food, but they would not believe me. They showed me Vichy-inspired articles and talked of what they heard on the radio. According to the French, the Germans were behaving extremely well. They were not taking food at all. What they were doing was to carry out what was called 'priority of purchase'. The Germans paid for what they took at a special rate of exchange, twenty francs to the mark.

From a French friend in Vichy I learned that Laval was working hard to kill the parliamentary régime in France. Herriot and Jeanneney had done all they could to oppose Laval but he had swung the majority of the Deputies and the Senators to his side. Only eighty members of the National Assembly had the courage to vote against the Pétain-Laval motion to wind up the Third French Republic. The actual date of the end was July 9th.

Georges Bonnet was also at Vichy holding Press conferences to prove that it was Great Britain that forced the war on France. Then I received a letter from the American Consul-

General in Marseilles saying he would be glad to receive me again, so back I went, but this time I had to go by rail, and what a difficult journey that was. I arrived in Montliémar early one morning and found it was practically impossible to get anything to eat. In the place where I went eventually there were a number of young Germans in civilian clothes. I listened to their conversation; it was all about butter and textiles. They talked of what they could buy. They talked of the French with good-natured contempt. When they went I said to the waitress: 'Do you get many Germans in here?' She said in a surprised tone of voice: 'Germans? We don't get any Germans.' I said to her: 'What about those who just went out?' She replied: 'They aren't Germans; they're Swiss. They told me so.'

When I reached Marseilles I found that plain-clothes detectives were blocking all the exits and making passengers show their papers and give an explanation as to why they had gone to Marseilles. People who could not give a convincing reason were not allowed to leave the station but had to return to their place of origin by the next available train. I had a hard time indeed. I showed a detective my letter from the American Consul and translated it for him. He answered me: 'He doesn't want to see you; he telephoned not to let any more through; he's got thousands of refugees to handle.'

I told the detective that I was not a refugee, so he asked me to show my return ticket, which of course I could not do, as I did not possess one. Then I showed him my passport and called attention to my exit visa. Actually, the visa had expired, but it said quite plainly that I was allowed to go to Spain via Marseilles. I hoped that the detective would not notice the time of the expired visa, and he did not, but he told me to go to Sete. I told him that was not possible, because I had to see the American Consul. Then I invited him to have a drink. We had a couple of drinks, and I got him talking about the wonderful French detective system. Then I shook hands with him, thanked him and left the station.

I went back to the Hotel Préfecture where I had stayed on my previous visit. There was a pretty girl behind the desk who told me that I could have a room but it would not be free until later. I left my rucksack in a corner and talked to the girl, who froze me when she said she hoped England would be bombed heavily, because the English were selfish people who always made others fight for them, and it was time England knew what war meant. I tried to reason with her, but then she told me that her husband was an officer in the French Navy, and was in a ship that had been fired on by the British. I went out in the darkened streets to try and get a meal and I ran into the man Fawcett again. This time he was in civilian clothes. He told me he had met a friend in the American Ambulance who, like himself, was also on the run, and his friend had a civilian suit of clothes, so they arranged to wear it in turns, day and day about. When I went back to the hotel, the proprietress, who was the mother of the pretty girl, was sitting behind the desk. I asked if my room was ready. She said to me: 'If I had known it was you, I wouldn't have let you have a room!' I asked her why, and she answered: 'Because you are English and the English are a band of cows; *ils me font chié!*' I picked up my rucksack and walked out of the hotel, and tried to get a room elsewhere, but it was impossible.

Then I went back to the Canebière, Marseilles' main street, and went to my old hotel, the Louvre et Paix, where I used to stay in pre-war days. Outside the hotel I noticed some French mobile guards. I went in and saw the reception clerk, who remembered me. I asked for a room, but he whispered behind his hand: 'You'd better get out of here; a German Armistice Commission of sixty has just arrived. They have taken the first three floors.'

At that moment an elderly man came up fussily and said he was an old client and must have a room. The clerk said there were no rooms free. The man said he must have a room; he could not sleep in the street. The clerk told the man to go outside, pick up a woman, and take her room. 'You needn't sleep with her', he explained. The old client began to splutter, but the dawn of understanding came into his eyes and he went out. Then I went on pressing for a room. The clerk wearily took a piece of paper, scribbled down an address, folded the paper and handed it to me. I asked where the place was and he said it was in the same street as the British Consulate. Again I went out into the darkness, and looked for the house, which I found in a very quiet street. At the top of a tall narrow staircase was the sort of *soubrette* that one used to see in musical comedies. I showed her the paper and asked for a room. She looked at it doubtfully and said: 'Madame isn't here yet.' I said I was tired of walking about and I just wanted to rest. She asked if I was alone, and I said yes, I was alone; I just wanted a single room. She took me to a rather gaudy room with a divan and three coloured photographs of girls in bathing costumes. Then she admonished me: 'You mustn't go to bed before Madame comes.' I said I would not and then she hovered at the door and said to me: 'You are an American, aren't you?' I told her that I was not American, that I was English. Then she asked me if I knew the Dolly Sisters. I told her, yes, I had met the Dolly Sisters. The maid said she used to be the Dolly Sisters' maid at Fontainbleau and had married the chauffeur.

I was terribly tired and I showed her how tired I was by yawning, and then I said I really must go to bed, but she told me very firmly that I could not go to bed until Madame arrived. She told me to go out for a walk, and I did. Then when I returned I found at the top of the stairs a well-dressed, perfumed, white marcelled-haired woman, who I presumed was Madame. There was also an unpleasant looking muscular man, counting huge piles of towels. Madame told me that if I rented the room I must guarantee not to return to it during the day and not to go to sleep before midnight. 'People come here to repose themselves during the day', she said sternly.

I went back to the room, took off my coat and sat down and began to write up my diary. Then I looked up and I noticed that one of the three coloured photographs of the girls in bathing costumes was missing. I thought I must be making a mistake, so I looked at the wall. Unmistakably a picture had hung there. I could not understand why it had disappeared, then the answer slowly dawned on me. But I slept very well, just the same.

In the morning early I went to the American Consulate, but obviously I was not there early enough, because there was already a queue of between three hundred and one thousand foreign refugees, each with a number stamped on a scrap of paper. I learned that many of them had been waiting day after day, all day, in the street, hoping to be able to get into the Consulate. With difficulty I managed to pass the gimlet-eyed janitor, and went upstairs to see the Consul. There once again I found Fawcett, who seemed to be entangled with a Polish girl who had a husband who had been arrested in Africa while trying to join the Foreign Legion. After a short conversation with the Consul, which did not help me very much, I left the Consulate with Fawcett and the girl. We went in a tram to a far-away suburb to see a wounded R.A.F. pilot who was hiding there. He eventually got away to England, where he wrote a book that sold extremely well. The tram ride was very embarrassing, because everywhere we went people stared at Fawcett. He explained: 'Because of my uniform; they think I am a German.' I kept telling the people that my friend was not a German, but they seemed merely politely amused. Then I understood why they were amused; they were amused at my innocence. They did not care one jot whether the man was a German or not. When I returned to the Hotel Louvre et Paix to tell the reception clerk what I thought of him, I found that the Germans were surrounded by a crowd and French women were making up to the German chauffeurs and were giving them flowers. I told the clerk that I was not going back to the bawdy house and I was going to have a room in his hotel. So he gave me a room in the servants' quarters and charged me a very fat figure for it.

I went back to the American Consulate, where I saw a slightly built fair-haired blue-eyed youngish-looking man in the garb of a British parson. I could not help noticing him because he was wearing one of those old-fashioned straw boater hats. He was the Reverend Donald Caskie, with whom I had a great deal more to do some time later. He had escaped from Paris where he had been in charge of the Scots Church. I must suppose that the pains Caskie suffered in Frèsnes prison must have impaired his memory, otherwise I cannot understand some of the matters he discusses in his book, *The Tartan Pimpernel*. Caskie says quite reverently that he was praying and he heard a Voice that directed him to the American Consulate in Marseilles, but from there he goes astray, and calls the American Consul-General Macfarlane, whereas the man who helped the Reverend Donald Caskie—and many, many British subjects—was John Hurley. Readers of *The Tartan Pimpernel* might reach a conclusion that I am sure Caskie does not wish to give, namely, that he and he alone assisted hundreds of British escaped prisoners of war to return to England. The Reverend Caskie was a link in the chain, but not the chain itself; without us others, the chain would not have functioned. His Seamen's Mission needed financing; it was financed as I relate a little later in this narrative.

The American Consul that day told me to go and see Major Dodds, who had been British Consul at Nice and whose absence had stranded thousands of his compatriots. Dodds said he went to Spain to help the Duke of Windsor to get to England. Despite the undoubted importance of that move, one is permitted perhaps to wonder why the flock of British Consuls in Spain were insufficient to help the Windsors to get away. But Dodds did return to France to work under the American Consul, and to try and help the British. Major Dodds before he went to Nice was Consul in Ethiopia and seemed to have curious ideas about his compatriots. I suppose it was so long since he had had to deal with any other than coloured people.

Then, in the middle of August, 1940, I went back to St Fortunat, because there was no way of getting a ship. Everywhere and all around me there was defeatism. I wondered where it was all going to end. My stock of money was running out, and I did not see any possibility of ever getting out of France. I went to Lyons and saw the American Consul there, a man named Stuart Allen, whom I had met in China. He advised me to go to the south of France, because, he said, if ever there was a ship, that was the only place I could get it. He told me that he could not give me a petrol permit; no doubt the French would not give me one either. The best thing I could do, he said, was to go to the Swedish Consulate, who were in charge of German interests. He indicated that I should say I wanted petrol to go forward to German-occupied territory. I went to the Swedish Consulate. The Consul was absent. He was a Frenchman. The Consulate was in the charge of his young son and a Nazi-hating Austrian young woman married to a Frenchman. I could see they did not believe my story, but they gave me a petrol permit. Allen also gave me a very impressive-looking letter in French to help me in case I had trouble with gendarmes on the route to Antibes, where I had made up my mind to go. That night I sat on the terrace of a café on the Place Bellecour, next to the Carlton Hotel in Lyons, where the German mission had its headquarters. The Germans' cold eyes appraised the sloppy French soldiers; several of them, like the civilians, were drunk. It was just like in Marseilles, when I was on the top floor of the hotel in the Canebière. In front of the hotel, showing off, French military police were pulling up French soldiers because they had their tunic buttons undone. Below me, members of the German mission were leaning their elbows on the window-sills, watching the passing show with a grin, like men watching a cage full of monkeys.

Chapter II

AT THE END OF AUGUST I was in Marseilles again en route to Antibes. This passage through the great Mediterranean city remains in my mind principally for one reason. I was watching the crowds outside the American Consulate hoping I might see someone I knew, and I did: an American journalist, Sam Dashiel from Paris, who had come from Bordeaux hoping to get to Algiers because, so he said, he was sure that one day the Allies would land in North Africa; it sounded crazy to me at the time. I never saw him again; he did not get to Algiers; he returned to America and during that country's occupation of Japan he died there, somewhat mysteriously. I went to live in a house on Cap d'Antibes, where two detectives called on me. I had written a letter to Robert Prew, the then editor of the *Daily Mail*, wherein I made use of the expression 'my plan', referring to a plan to do some work. The letter had been intercepted and opened. The detectives, quite friendly really, wanted to know what I meant. One of the detectives, Meslin, came from the Paris Sûreté; he was married to a Jewess and was pro-Ally. He told me there were constant reports of an abortive German invasion of Britain; he said there were stories of thousands of partially burned bodies of Germans washed up on the French Channel coast.

A day or so later I was walking on the promenade towards Cannes, watching the many French goods trains travelling towards Italy; there were Italian soldiers on the box cars and on the flat-top trucks, although this was unoccupied France. While I was watching, a man accosted me and asked if I spoke English; he was bare-headed; he wore an open-necked shirt and a light-coloured suit. His hair was curly, his lips thick. When he walked beside me, he walked in the gutter; he took long strides, his head bent, he swung his arms in half circles, his hands open, palms downwards. I noticed he had a small scar near one corner of his mouth. I had seen hundreds of coloured men in Africa walk just that way. I asked him if he was a

South African and he said he was; his name he said was Wilson and he was in the Royal Engineers. He claimed he was in hiding up in the mountains at Sospel. He asked me to help him get to England; I asked him why he should think I could do that. He shrugged: 'I thought you could.' I was a bit worried about this, so I went on to Cannes and saw Inspector Meslin, one of the already-named detectives who had called on me, and who was stationed there. When I told my little story he asked: 'Has the man a scar on his mouth?' When I said he had, he said: 'Be careful, he is a provocative agent.'

On September 7th, I saw painted in red on the pavement in the Avenue Wilson the words: 'Down With The Jews!' Stuck up outside the Pam-Pam bar were posters attacking the Jews, saying they were both buyers and sellers in the Black Market. But the real local profiteers on the local Black Market were the 'White' Russians, of whom there was a large colony, and the Italians; the Russians found the goods and the Italians sold them.

The food situation grew rapidly worse now; horse meat for human consumption was rationed just like other meat. Nominally the ration was 270 grammes of meat per person per week, with bone, but in reality meat was only procurable on Saturdays, and then one had to start queueing up at seven a.m.; by nine-thirty a.m. there was no more.

I made an arrangement to receive £26 per month at the pre-war rate of exchange from the British Consulate at Nice. After the Consulate staff left the Consulate was nominally in the charge of the American Consulate, but actually it was run by the most extraordinary crew of Britishers, all of whom clung to their first war ranks. But there were others, John Amery for instance, who was later hanged for treason. While hundreds of his compatriots were on the breadline because their country's representatives had stranded them, John Amery was receiving £50 per month. After serving prison sentences in Britain, he ran away from his wife in England and went to live with a harlot in Nice. Then there was a queer limping captain who had understudied the original Fred Emney in

London; a Captain Chadwick, now dead, who was a scion of the famous Lancashire cotton family. He had a fine voice, had sung in opera, and after the war sang in the chorus of the Monte Carlo Opera. Then there was a man who called himself a colonel, but who turned out to be an absconding bookmaker from Penang.

When the war reached the French Riviera, it found it totally unprepared. The Carlton Hotel, Cannes, like its near neighbour, Martinez, appeared to be doing very well, despite the fact that the France one knew was dead. The Sporting Club was closed, but the big Municipal Casino also appeared to be doing very well; Monsieur André was living in Cannes looking after his property. All the big hotels remained open. The Carlton Hotel, as usual, was patronised by the cosmopolitan set, and was a mare's nest of rumour. It was a poor day when, amongst others, Prince Andrew of Greece did not have something really sensational to circulate, such as the assassination of King Leopold of Belgium, or maybe the violent death of Laval.

Nicolas Titulescu, the former Rumanian Premier, lived at the Carlton and he died there during the early days of the armistice. Not long before he died he sent me a note asking me how much money he would be able to obtain for writing articles for the United States. He said he was trying to get to Brazil, but his money was locked up in Switzerland.

Monsieur Titulescu in Cannes, and for some years previous, had as a sort of bodyguard an Englishman, an ex-soldier. During the last days of Titulescu's life, the bodyguard's principal duty was to go about seeking the morphia that Titulescu was in the habit of injecting into himself. The real cause of Titulescu's death was gangrene, set up by the hypodermic needles which I presume were not sufficiently clean.

Among the other colourful patrons of the Carlton Hotel was the late E. Phillips Oppenheim, who will no doubt be remembered by older readers as one of the greatest tale-spinners of their youth and middle age. He amassed an enormous fortune and settled down to live in a very pleasant house on the French Riviera, but although he was not by any means what one might call a young man, he had innumerable French mistresses dotted about the landscape. He had a large car and an English chauffeur. Oppenheim would say: 'Tom, I think this afternoon we'll drive over and see Madame X. No, wait a minute, Tom, surely, no, wait a minute. No, let's go over and see Madame D.' But according to Tom, the list was quite a lengthy one. At this period E. Phillips Oppenheim, the late Lord Furness, and Baron Fritz von Thyssen tried to charter a yacht which belonged to the ex-Khedive of Egypt, who was de-throned, with the aid of the Aga Khan, during the first world war. The ex-Khedive had been living in Switzerland but he spent some considerable part of the year in France and was in Cannes when the war broke out. The trio started offering the ex-Khedive large sums of money to charter the yacht in order to try and get away to England. Eventually they offered him a million francs. The ex-Khedive laughed. 'I don't want money', he said. 'The British Government pays me £30,000 a year, income tax free.' Not long after this incident, Lord Furness died in Cannes; the French handed over the German Baron to the Germans; Phillips Oppenheim eventually managed to get away to England, but he did not stay there long; he only stayed until the end of the war and then he moved to the Channel Isles, to Jersey I think it was, where he died. He was always very wary of British income tax.

It was about this time that I ran into my Paris tailor, an Irishman named McSweeney. He told me how he and his French wife and daughter escaped from Paris in a closed hearse. There was another incident in which a hearse was concerned. An Englishwoman died in Cannes and had requested that her body be cremated. Her husband, anxious to fall in with the wishes of the deceased, set about trying to find out how in wartime it was possible to be cremated, but he discovered that there was no crematorium nearer than Marseilles. He chartered a motor-hearse and a driver, and sitting next to the driver, with the coffin inside the hearse, he set out for Marseilles, but when he arrived there, he found that owing to war-time restrictions, the crematorium was only open during certain hours of the day, so he left the coffin at the crematorium until it was open, and then he and the driver went and spent the afternoon at the cinema.

Then there was the case of Mr Hope-Johnstone, an eighty-three-year-old British millionaire, who died at the Carlton Hotel shortly after sending Mr Winston Churchill a cheque for £15,000 to help win the war. In his will the millionaire said that his body was to be embalmed and sent to Switzerland for burial. The dead man had been connected with the firm of Morgan Grenfell, so the American Consulate in Nice took charge of the matter, and, on account of the importance of the banking house with which the dead man had been connected, the State Department in Washington came into the matter, and just as if there had been no war at all, there were cables passing to and fro concerning the minute instructions that the dead millionaire had left behind him. After many headaches on the part of the American Consul, the body was placed in the vault of the English church in Nice until the end of the war.

People, particularly the poorer people, were very hard hit; there was an epidemic of petty crimes, mostly thieving. Rabbits and chickens disappeared from gardens. There was no fuel, and although in pre-war days I had passed many winter weeks in the sunny south, I had always stayed in hotels where there was plenty of heat, but now there was none, and when one has no food in one's belly, one feels the cold intensely. I used to see poorly-clad humans going through the dust-bins, searching for food, and next to them were lean, hungry dogs, who had been turned loose by their masters who could no longer manage to feed them. Dogs and humans fought side by side for such crumbs as might have dropped from the rich men's tables.

Petrol was rationed, and as the fishing-boats were practically all motor-boats, they depended naturally on the petrol ration in order to be able to go to sea, but they did not go to sea. The fishermen found it paid them better to sell their petrol in the Black Market rather than go to sea to catch fish, so fish was at a premium, and meat, except for the very rich who could afford to dabble in the Black Market, was unobtainable.

In those pretty gardens which adjoin the Cannes Casino, there used to be two marble statues. One was of Edward VII in yachting costume. Both King Edward VII and his mother Queen Victoria had been great patrons of the French Riviera. The good Cannois, in order to show their appreciation, smashed this statue to smithereens. In another corner of the gardens was a marble bust of Lord Brougham, who not only gave his name to a special type of carriage, but who was the man who turned Cannes from a small fishing village into a prosperous Riviera resort. Once again the local inhabitants showed their appreciation. They smashed this piece of marble to smithereens also.

It was not more than a few days later that I went back to the room I was occupying in the villa on the Cap d'Antibes when I casually noticed a green bicycle propped up against the wall. I went up to my room and I was told that a young Englishman had come to see me. I went into another room, where I saw a fair young man who told me that he was an officer in the Durham Light Infantry; his name was Lieutenant Martin. He said he had been taken prisoner in the early part of the campaign, actually in Boulogne, and had managed to make his escape.

'How did you get away?' I asked.

'Oh, I just "won" a bicycle.'

A cold suspicion entered my mind. 'What sort of bicycle?' I asked.

'It was a green bicycle', the young man answered. Then I realised only too well that it was the bicycle that was outside propped up against the wall. I kept him under cover and got into touch with Inspector Meslin, who procured forged French papers for him and I got my young English friend away to Marseilles, where I passed him on to the Reverend Donald Caskie, to whom I have already introduced you, and that incident was my casual introduction to what became known as the Resistance. In a very short space of time, the young man was back in his regiment.

Then there was the case of another man who turned up. I will call him O'Dash. He said to me as a conversational gambit: 'You needn't be afraid of me; I know you got so-and-so away. I want you to get me away.' I had not the faintest idea of what to do. Would it be possible once again to apply for the good offices of my French detective friend, I wondered. My second visitor was the adjutant of a battalion of a very famous regiment. I was afraid that he might have been planted on me by the French, because a little time previously, as I have related, a man who turned out to be a provocative agent had contacted me. But O'Dash was a very different proposition. He very quickly proved to me that he had done some journalistic work and that he was a great friend of one of the executives of a national newspaper in London, of whose staff I had been a member for a good many years. When O'Dash escaped from the Germans he wrote to Sean Murphy, the Irish Minister at Vichy, and said in his letter that he was an Irish journalist who had lost his passport. He said he was born in Cork. Back came an Irish passport, so O'Dash was able to travel into unoccupied territory in very good style. I was able to get him away just as I got the other one away, but then things began to get more and more difficult.

A gendarme left a pink paper with my landlady. I had to report immediately at Antibes police station. I found a number of English people being kept waiting on the pavement; also an Irishman who had been arrested while on holiday; he had an Eire passport but no identity papers, so he was kept in prison for a month without trial, and then they fined him 2,000 francs and made him pay the cost of his imprisonment! After being kept waiting outside on the pavement I was interviewed like a criminal. I was asked what I was doing in France; what were my means; why was I in Antibes? I said I was waiting to get a ship to take me to Britain. The inspector laughed.

'The Germans are sinking all the British ships', he said. Then he added: 'You have no money; you will have to go to a concentration camp.' I produced £10 in British currency. His eyes glistened. I had to think and act quickly.

'I have a friend in London who has just retired from Scotland Yard and is going to open a private detective agency after the war. He asked me to look out for a Frenchman to represent him in this country. Do you know of anybody? Perhaps you, yourself . . . he would pay well, in English money, of course.'

Without batting an eyelid, he wrote me out a permit to remain in Antibes for three months. He did not know how much I needed that piece of paper. The Spanish Government had, in fact, notified me that I could not be granted a transit visa.

Chapter III

THE REFUSAL OF A transit visa across Spain combined with what I now accepted as the impossibility of finding transport by sea to Britain or to any port from which I could re-ship to Britain made me reconsider my position once again, as it now was. If I could not reach London, what could I do in France? The answer to my personal problem was nearer than I knew. I had heard tell of a clandestine office in Cannes, where there were people, so it was said, who helped stranded British subjects; the place was located in what in pre-war days were the offices of the firm of John Taylor, the estate agents on the Croisette. I made my way there.

I found the office held down by a Mr George Grounsell, a former British Vice-Consul in Naples. When Italy entered the war, Grounsell and his wife found their way to Cannes, where Grounsell made the acquaintance of Sir Coleridge Kennard. Some two years later Grounsell and I, separately, made our way to Lisbon, where Grounsell died of tuberculosis; Kennard, after a period of solitary confinement in Frèsnes prison, where the Reverend Donald Caskie also spent a spell, was interned, as was Caskie, in St Denis; shortly after the end of the war, Kennard died in France; of our little group, the originators of the escape route for members of the British Forces, Caskie and myself are the only survivors.

Kennard I had known slightly in Paris, where he had a flat. His father was the founder of the *Evening News* and contributed very largely to the Tory Party funds. He made a vast amount of money, but not out of the *Evening News*, and with part of his fortune he purchased large estates in the south of France chiefly on Cap Ferrat. Sir Coleridge had a small house in Cannes, just at the back of the Carlton Hotel. In fact the Carlton Hotel tennis courts, famous in their day, were his property. Sir Coleridge was a member of the British Diplomatic Service, but he was also a poet and a writer of no mean talent. He left the Diplomatic Service because of ill health and spent his time between Cannes and Paris. At the time I met up with him again he was a widower.

Sir Coleridge was doing his best to help his less fortunately situated compatriots, some two thousand of whom were stranded in various parts of the Riviera, owing, as I have told, to the British Consulates having hurried off and burnt all their records. But out of this charitable beginning, Sir Coleridge, with the aid of Grounsell, built up an organisation that in the beginning enabled many members of the Forces to return to Britain and join up again; then, when I came into the picture, we obtained items of vital information which Kennard transmitted to London; I was the 'undercover' man; I seldom showed up in the Cannes office, which, until the Americans closed us down, was maintained as a 'front'. As shrewd as we no doubt thought we were, the Germans were lucky enough to have planted, right in our office, a Miss Smart, an Anglo-German who, when the war ended, was put on trial by the French and met with a just fate. There was, however, an incident early on which should have warned us.

Miss Smart's late father had kept a small hotel in Cannes; her mother was German. Miss Smart at this time was in her early forties; she was heftily built and very Teutonic in appearance; she spoke English, French and German. Among the things that Sir Coleridge was doing, a job in which I was helping as best I could, was collecting from various people articles of clothing for the British troops who had escaped from German camps in occupied territory and who had managed to get into unoccupied territory, only to be interned by the French in the Fort at Marseilles which I have already mentioned. Before they could escape back to Britain they needed civilian clothing very badly indeed, because it was a very cold winter. I happened to have with me a spare pair of heavy brogues, one of two pairs which I had used a year before when I had spent the winter tramping the jungles of Liberia. And I had a pair of flannel trousers, a spare pair; although I loathed to part with such treasures, I knew they could be used for a very good purpose. Such clothing as I managed to collect was kept in a room above the office. I happened to go upstairs to put some other things there when I noticed that my brogues and my flannel trousers had disappeared. I came down and told Grounsell, who said in an embarrassed tone of voice: 'I think Miss Smart knows something about them, don't you, Miss Smart?'

Without any sort of embarrassment at all, Miss Smart said: 'I took them to give to a young German.'

'What young German?' I asked, rather sharply, I suppose.

'Oh, to a young German I happened to see outside. The poor boy was shivering and very badly clothed.'

'Do you mean to say he was an escaped prisoner?'

'Yes', replied Miss Smart, 'I suppose he was, but what's that got to do with it?'

Well, there was nothing more that I could say, so I did not say any more, but like the sailor's parrot, I thought a lot, and it certainly occurred to me how dangerous it was to have a person like Miss Smart around. When I saw Sir Coleridge I put that point to him, but he said in his tolerant way that it was difficult to get anybody to work at that moment; he would, however, keep an eye on Miss Smart.

When some time later he was picked up and sent to 'enforced residence' in Grenoble, he took Miss Smart along with him so that she could do secretarial work. He not only paid her but he also paid for her board and lodging. He said to me facetiously: 'She eats like a Prussian Grenadier.' Then I discovered that she was dabbling in the Black Market; I kept that to myself.

In appearance Kennard looked like the typical stage British diplomat. He was very tall and very thin; he wore a rimless monocle attached to a thick black cord, and he had a drooping nether lip. He was proud of being an Old Etonian and always wore an Old Etonian tie and Old Etonian cuff-links. But he he had a very shrewd brain. One day Coleridge came into the office and said: 'There's a woman sitting on a chair on the landing out there who looks just like Queen Victoria.' Miss Smart looked up from her typewriter and said: 'That's my mother!' I went outside to have a look, and there sure enough sat an old lady in black with a sort of antimacassar on her head, and she *did* look like the known portraits of Queen Victoria. But Miss Smart undoubtedly did put the Germans on to the track of Sir Coleridge Kennard.

One Sunday afternoon a horse-cab stopped outside Sir Coleridge's house. The housekeeper, Miss Barnet (who became the third Lady Kennard and died of tuberculosis a few months before her husband) opened the door. There stood a well-dressed young woman.

'Are you Lady Kennard?' the visitor enquired. Miss Barnet

said she was not. The woman at the door said she had just come from Marseilles where Major Dodds had told her to go to Cannes to see Sir Coleridge Kennard. At that time the Major, as I have related, had been sent back to Marseilles to help the American Consul there. At that moment Sir Coleridge Kennard came downstairs and saw the woman and asked if she had a note or some sort of introduction from Major Dodds. She said she had nothing. Sir Coleridge asked her to come inside and there then proceeded this very extraordinary conversation. Sir Coleridge asked the lady to sit down and said: 'What can I do for you?'

The woman answered: 'I want you to help me to get to Spain; I must go to San Sebastian, at once; I have an appointment there with a German officer who is going to give me the German plans for the Spring offensive. From San Sebastian I can get to Lisbon and from there to England.'

'But, my dear lady', answered Sir Coleridge, 'this is fantastic; I may be interned myself at any moment. I have no power or authority to help you to get to Spain. That is a matter for the Americans, the French, and the Spanish authorities.'

'Yes, but listen; I've got to get to San Sebastian; I know you have helped people over the frontier.'

'Quite untrue, madame. I must ask you to leave.'

'Listen, Sir Coleridge, my husband works in the War Office in London. Before the war I was staying in Biarritz with my mother. Just before the war started my husband wrote and told me to keep my eyes open. One day when I was on a picnic party I made a sketch of a French aerodrome. When the Germans entered Biarritz they arrested me and found the sketch. I was put in prison. While I was in prison I was visited by a German officer who told me that he was an anti-Nazi. He said that if I could get out of France, he would meet me in San Sebastian and give me the plans for the Spring offensive.'

'But, my dear lady, Biarritz is practically next door to San Sebastian. Why did you have to go to Marseilles and then come here?'

'Well, this is the point; while I was in prison, the Gestapo came to see me and said they would release me, if I would do a job of spying for them.'

'So you are doing it?'

'No, of course not—may I smoke? But unless you get me out of this country I shall have to, or go back to prison.'

'I see; but tell me, how did you manage to cross the line of demarcation?'

'Oh, I bribed one of the French officials to get me false papers. I paid him ten thousand francs.'

'Oh, the Germans allowed you to handle money, then?'

'I'm not short of money. Look!' Then, according to Sir Coleridge, she fumbled in her clothing and brought out a large packet of thousand franc notes.

'I'm sorry', went on Sir Kennard, 'but I can't help you. Indeed, I think you had better be going now.'

'Let me sleep here tonight?'

'That's impossible.'

'Anywhere will do; this sofa!'

'I'm sorry; no!'

Sir Coleridge said that the woman argued and argued and then he got up, went towards his study and rang for a servant to see the woman out. The cab was still at the door. The woman was heard to tell the driver to go to the station. Miss Barnet, whose suspicions had been aroused, was already holding a servant to hurry out to see which way the cab went. The cab did not go to the station; it went to the Carlton Hotel. Kennard asked me what I made of the story. My first theory was that the woman was a provocative agent employed by the French, but Kennard himself was equally sure that she was a German agent. He recalled that in the first world war he had been closely connected with a certain British Service in Sweden. He was then *en poste* at Stockholm. He recalled how clumsy the Germans had been with their spies. I asked Sir Coleridge if the woman was good-looking. Apparently she was very good-looking and very attractive. After some more conversation, Kennard suggested that if I would be willing to take the risk, I should go over to Marseilles and try and make enquiries from Major Dodds. This I agreed to do.

But even in those tragic days there was occasional light relief. This is an instance of what I mean. On the Carlton Hotel tennis courts before the war there was a professional coach, a Captain Cyril Upton. He was a nice-looking fellow, an old Pauline, who in the first world war had been a physical instructor with the R.F.C., hence no doubt the title of captain. After the war, he went to India, where he became a tennis coach to several Maharajahs. Then he returned to the South of France, where he became a tennis coach and he was also the Cannes correspondent of *The Times*. He was also a poet, and wrote, and I am told by those who know far better than I, that he was a very good poet, and it was through his poetry no doubt that he came into contact with Sir Coleridge Kennard, and it was at Sir Coleridge's house that I met him. I was horrified—and let me once again remind you that all this took place after the fall of France—I was horrified, I say, by his defeatist attitude and by his anti-British propaganda. He said at the luncheon table, for example, that B.B.C. news bulletins were 'all lies'. Then he repeated what so many French people were saying at that time, that President Roosevelt's name was really Rosenfeld, and that he was a renegade Jew, and so on.

Although Sir Coleridge was one hundred per cent British and pro-British and all that those words mean, yet his love for poetry made him forgive the things that Upton was saying, and even caused him to smile tolerantly at some of the things Upton did. For instance, soon after the outbreak of war, Upton persuaded himself and his friends that he would be appointed Provost Marshal—British Provost Marshal, of course —for that part of France. So to that end, and while waiting for his appointment, he bought himself a very nice British uniform. Then he thought that his equipment was incomplete, so he bought himself a sword. Then came Dunkirk, and being a thorough defeatist, Upton thought that Britain was about to throw in her hand, so he cut up his uniform and burnt it. But one cannot cut up a sword and burn that, and Captain Cyril Upton was very much afraid that if he was caught with a sword, things might go badly with him. So he buried the sword in the garden of the villa where he was living.

Every Thursday afternoon, Sir Coleridge Kennard and Captain Cyril Upton shut themselves up in the living-room of Sir Coleridge's house and would hold a sort of poetry-*fest*. They would read to one another verses they had written. But when Upton read some of his pieces, it would cause him to weep, and even if he repeated the same piece Thursday after Thursday, he would nevertheless weep.

What became of Captain Cyril Upton, you may want to know? Well, I cannot tell you the whole history because it would take up too much space. He obtained a certain amount of financial assistance from Sir Coleridge Kennard and then he tried to persuade a young English girl who had been doing some secretarial work for him to write to his wife, who had gone back to England, to say that he could not join her there because he was engaged on British Secret Service work. In fact, he was having a very pleasant time indeed in the south of France, and particularly in Cannes, but a little later, Sir Coleridge and many others of Sir Coleridge's compatriots, including myself, were rounded up and sent into forced residence. But not Captain Cyril Upton. Oh dear, no. He obtained financial assistance elsewhere and somehow managed to escape the Vichy French dragnet. This continued for some time, but not for the whole time. Towards the end of the war, he was rounded up by the Germans, after the Germans had occupied the part of France that at the beginning of the armistice was unoccupied. Captain Cyril Upton, accompanied by many trunks full of suits of clothes, was dumped into the internment camp for British civilian prisoners at St Denis, on the northern outskirts of Paris. He arrived, so I was told later by Sir Coleridge who was also there, calling aloud for the intervention of Marshal Pétain. But his cries remained unanswered. He stayed in that camp until the end of the war; even then his native wit did not desert him, because he soon appointed himself a war correspondent, and wore a war correspondent's uniform.

At that time we were getting very little news of the Reverend Donald Caskie, but recently he has written his own version of what was happening at his end of the escape chain. Dr Caskie, a doctor of divinity, relates how he was put on trial and given a sentence of two years, 'avec souris', as he calls it, which in English would mean 'with mice'; this did not mean he was to be put into a dungeon where there were mice. He says he asked the judge what it meant; I am surprised that the Reverend Caskie, who had lived so long in Paris, did not understand. What the judge said in reality was: 'avec sursis'; in other words, a suspended sentence. He did not get committed to jail, fortunately for the members of the Forces we were passing on to him.

Chapter IV

ON MANY WALLS and hoardings between Cannes and Nice there were now posters saying that General de Gaulle was nothing but a creature of the Jews; to be a supporter of de Gaulle meant that one was supporting the Jews. Across the pavements of Nice and Cannes and in Antibes were slogans in large white letters: 'Down With The Jews', and 'Death To The Jews'. In Nice, there was not only anti-Semite jealousy but right along the façade of the British church was written in whitewash the words: 'Death To Churchill'. It is perhaps unkind of me to mention those things today, but for my part

I think that they should not be forgotten. It was now really dangerous for English people to talk English one to the other in public. In Antibes there was living an old English lady, the wife of a baronet. She had been very good to the French poor of the neighbourhood and had given quite large sums of money to various local charities. Yet, one day when she was getting off an omnibus in what used to be called the Place Macé but which was now re-named the Place Maréchal Pétain, the conductor pushed her off the step with great brutality and shouted: 'Get off, you old English cow!' I had to spend a great deal of time around the centre of Antibes about that time, because there was much information to be picked up there. For instance, I discovered in Antibes harbour five small corvettes the French had built for Franco, and which were rusting away, but now they were being repaired for German use in the Mediterranean. Ye Olde Shippe Bar on the Place Macé was the meeting place of curious people, collaborationists and German fellow-travellers. There was the late Norman Douglas; his friend, a Danish artist named Christian; Fort, a French painter; Adams, an American remittance man; Wilcox, a wealthy American, and his German 'secretary'; and several French counts who had served in the defeated French Army. The barman was Austrian-born, and so was his wife. There were also some Russians, a man named Stark, and a girl known as Toucha who was the wife of a French prisoner of war and the mistress of the young Count de Martel, who was the head of the local branch of the so-called Legion that Pétain intended to be his private army, but which Laval turned into a Fascist militia. Martel lost an arm in the war; that did not prevent him leading the Legion gang in forays to break up Jewish-owned shops. The curious part was that the Count de Martel is half-Jewish by birth; his mother was born a Jewess and was converted. It was nauseating to hear the Count praising the *tenue* of some passing Italian officers, but the limit so far as I was concerned was reached when I heard Count de Martel and his friend talking like this:

'Did you know that our Division is allowed to wear the Iron Cross?'

'No, I didn't know.'

'Yes, Hitler has decreed that our Division fought so bravely, we are allowed to wear the German Iron Cross.'

Since the Liberation of France, Count de Martel's amputated arm has given him adequate protection.

Personal relations became strained. There was a Luxembourgoise woman I had known before the war, the widow of a French officer who was killed in the first war; she was now living in Antibes. I discovered that during the previous summer she had met a couple whom she suspected of being Fifth Columnists; now she had written to them to their Paris address seeking their help in obtaining permission to go herself to Paris; she had also been in personal touch with the German Armistice Commissioner in Nice! Another citizen of Luxembourg, Pierre Wolf, whom I mentioned in an earlier chapter, drove up to my lodgings one evening in a pony chaise; he was living on the large estate he had bought for Paternôtre. He said quite frankly that he would not risk visiting me in the day-time but he had come to warn me that the police were watching me. But such risks as I might have been running at that time were not calculated risks; things seemed to happen to me.

By the end of October, 1940, the food situation was awful. I had to toast the soggy bread, otherwise it was uneatable; potatoes had vanished. I used to think back to the splendid meals I had eaten in pre-war winters along the coast; the gentle breezes and soft music; the nights filled with stars and a crescent moon. There would be light laughter while strolling in and out of the casinos. Now all there was to eat were stewed crows, a little horse-meat, or none; swedes, *rutabagas* and some edible weeds. The cats turned wild and took to the woods; dogs were lean, gaunt and hungry, turned off by their owners who could no longer feed themselves. I wondered why the municipality did not have the dogs put out of their misery.

God, how cold it was. I went down with a bout of malaria. Then, the first time I went out, I met with two adventures.

My clothes were shabby and I was often unshaven; I wore an old *béret*. On this day my appearance no doubt saved my liberty, and maybe more. There were constant rumours of the total occupation of France and vague rumours of the presence of British agents; I had questioned Kennard, but he gave non-committal replies. This day I walked slowly, I was so weak, over to La Garoupe, a small nearby beach. I had walked over to the lighthouse at the edge of the Cape and then down to La Garoupe, where I had made some friendly contacts which I thought vaguely might possibly be useful. This day there was no one there. I had the beach completely to myself. I sat on the rocks and looked idly out to sea. Nothing to be seen. Then I saw coming round the corner of the rocky cape a small rubber dinghy; in it sat a man who was paddling it. I looked on, very surprised. The man clutched hold of a rock and pulled himself in; then he looked up and about very carefully, but he did not see me. He climbed out of the dinghy and held on to the edge. He leaned over and did something that at first I could not see; then I noticed that he was using one hand to fill the dinghy with stones. I presumed he then sunk it; the water is very deep at the edge of the rocks. Then I saw he was taking off his waders. I thought he would fill those with sea water; I guessed without knowing how that this man for some reason wanted to get rid of anything that would connect him with the dinghy. I did not want him to see me watching, so while he was occupied with his waders, I slipped as quietly as I could off the left side of the rocks so as to reach the sandy beach. I stretched myself out and pretended to be sleeping. In a moment or so I heard his footfalls on the sand. I rolled myself over and sat up like a man just wakening from a doze. He looked at me in no way surprised and I tried to keep all surprise out of my face. He said: 'Bon jour', and I replied: 'Bon jour'. His accent was good, very good indeed, but no matter how well an Englishman talks a foreign language I can myself speak I know instinctively that he is an Englishman. But would he detect my accent, I wondered? I asked him no questions and hoped he would think I was just a Frenchman unemployed because of the war; there were plenty such. I longed to say: 'I'm English, like you; can I help?' But I dared not. We exchanged a few words and then he walked on unhurriedly. I waited about ten or fifteen minutes and then I started back to my lodgings.

I was not far from the house when I saw two motor-cars loaded up with German officers in uniform coming towards me; they were led as those German convoys always were, by a 'pioneer' car with a French flag. This car was being driven by a French sailor, and there was a French naval officer and a French army officer sitting in the back. It was a lonely stretch of road. When the 'pioneer' car was alongside me, it stopped and the carloads of Germans stopped too. So did my heart, or so it seemed.

The sailor-driver beckoned to me and I walked across. 'Can you tell me the way to the lighthouse?' the driver asked. I could hear the Germans muttering and noticed they were looking annoyed; I guessed the reason; they thought the French were playing them some trick. But before I could answer the driver's question, the door of the nearer German car opened and a big hefty Hun got out and walked over and stood right next to me. I hoped my accent would hold good.

'*Deux cents mètres plus loin et à gauche*', I said, as nonchalantly as I could. I touched my *béret* in farewell as a Frenchman would, and walked slowly on my way, anxiously listening for the cars to get into gear.

At about this time I received a letter smuggled out of Paris. It told me that Hitler paid a secret visit to Paris in the previous September and had been taken to see the interior of the Opera House at six in the morning! The Swastika was flying from all public buildings, including the Eiffel Tower and the Arc de Triomphe. The Opéra opened for the first time since France

E*

fell. *The Damnation of Faust* was the opera chosen for the re-opening, and the audience was practically wholly German, uniformed officers and civilians. The Opera House functioned like the German theatres; performances began at six-thirty p.m. and finished at eight forty-five p.m. There were at that time thousands of closed shops in Paris and whole streets with either the curtains drawn or the shutters shut. Hungry dogs haunted the streets, looking for food and their lost masters. There were neither taxis nor omnibuses then; the Paris Metropolitan was running fitfully, but the lifts and moving staircases were not working. The bakers' and grocers' shops were open mornings only. There was a considerable movement of German troops and material. The Germans had made the Paris firemen remove all British and French flags still flying in Paris. The German military headquarters were in the Ministry of Marine, at the corner of the rue Royale.

All that information was subsequently relayed to London. Was it useful? Well, eventually the Ministry of Marine was bombed by R.A.F. bombers; 'one of our bombers was missing'. Some of the crew landed alive on the roof of the Magasins du Louvre, about a quarter of a mile from the Ministry of Marine.

News from Vichy was scarce at this time, but towards the end of October Laval met Hitler and Ribbentrop in Paris; Ribbentrop also met Franco. The Laval-Hitler meeting had sensational repercussions a little less than two months later.

In December it was announced that Pétain had dropped Laval from his Cabinet and replaced him with Flandin. What really happened was that Pétain had placed Laval under arrest. This is what happened.

Laval returned from the meeting with Hitler on December 13th. Laval arranged with Hitler that Pétain was to go to a ceremony to take place at Napoleon's Tomb in the Invalides. The remains of Napoleon's son, '*L'Aiglon*', were to be brought from Vienna and placed in his father's tomb. But Laval had plotted to have Pétain held as a hostage in Paris so that he could replace him in Vichy. Hitler had asked Laval to attack

French overseas territories then in the hands of General de Gaulle's Free French; to recruit soldiers for the French Army; to start up making munitions for Germany with coal and raw materials supplied by Germany; to rearm French ships and build aeroplanes. French technicians held in German prison camps were to be released for that purpose. Laval said he would carry out those propositions but Pétain never would. But Pétain's spies had informed him of Laval's plot to make him a prisoner. As soon as Laval returned to Vichy from Paris, Pétain called a Ministerial Cabinet meeting which was held at eight-thirty in the evening of December 13th. Pétain asked all the Ministers to hand in their resignations. When they were all in his hands Pétain said: 'I'll retain two: that of Ribert (who was Minister of Public Instruction and in the plot with Laval) and Pierre Laval's.'

Laval then left the meeting and went to dine at the Hotel du Parc with Fernand de Brinon. It was Laval's intention to drive back to Paris that night, so towards the end of dinner he sent for his chauffeur. A message came back that his chauffeur was under arrest. Laval then went to his office, which was in the hotel. While he was there detectives came in saying they had orders to take Laval to his estate at Chateldon, about sixteen miles from Vichy. Laval left with the detectives. He was under house arrest for three days; he was not allowed the use of the telephone, nor was he allowed to contact anyone outside the house. Hitler sent his personal representative in Paris, Otto Abetz, to Vichy. Abetz saw Pétain and then went to see Laval, who was released immediately. Abetz saw Pétain again and then left for Paris by road.

On Saturday, January 18th, Laval left his estate and went to La Ferté Haute-Rive, which is near Moulins, about forty miles north of Vichy. He wrote twice to Pétain; on receipt of the second letter Pétain went to see Laval. He then issued an official statement saying that all misunderstandings had been cleared up.

Then in January, 1941, Sir Coleridge Kennard asked me to

undertake a mission to Marseilles, a mission with a double purpose: to obtain certain information concerning what was happening in Marseilles and to take a large sum of money to the Reverend Donald Caskie, to finance the Marseilles end of the escape route. The money came through from the War Office in rather a curious way. Herman Rogers, a great friend of the Duke of Windsor, was living in Cannes. He was an American subject and America was not yet in the war, so Americans could receive monies from the United States. It was Herman Rogers who received the money and handed it to Sir Coleridge, who handed it to me, warning me of the risks of my mission, leaving the details to me, but saying, as one is always told, that he did not want to know anything about it, because he could accept no responsibility.

I went to Antibes police station and said the American Consul in Marseilles wanted to see me about getting me a visa to leave France; with an air of innocence I asked if I needed a permit to go to Marseilles. I asked how long it would take for my permit to come through, and was told it would be a week to ten days. I expressed my gratitude and said I would telegraph to the Consul to say it would be at least a week before I could be in Marseilles. The Consul must have been surprised to receive my telegram, because my visit was purely imaginary; it was my alibi; if I was caught without a permit—I was not in the least likely to be granted one—then I would say that the Consul could not wait until the permit came through, so I had to take a chance.

My first anxiety on my arrival in Marseilles was to find a place to lodge, and I struck lucky the first time. I recalled a Hotel Colbert, behind the Bourse; it faced a large piece of waste ground that was the hang-out of tramps and other vagrants. When I went in I dropped my rucksack on the floor and asked for a room. The woman behind the desk looked at me shrewdly for a moment.

'In a spot of trouble, dearie?' she asked. 'You need not register.' Before I could even think of an answer she turned and took a key off a hook behind her, and handed it to me. 'Number twenty-four, dearie; you'll be all right here.'

At that time, the Fort St Jean at Marseilles, which was the Foreign Legion prison, held more than four hundred members of the British Armed Forces who had been prisoners of war of the Germans but who had escaped from German prison camps in occupied France. Donald Caskie had re-opened the Seamen's Home in Marseilles and was doing all he could for the British prisoners in Fort St Jean; his cousin, also a Reverend Caskie, had been a padre with the 53rd Lowland Division in France. Donald Caskie needed money to carry on his work; the Seamen's Home was his 'front'; the money I had with me in French banknotes was sewn up in the clothes I wore. The morning after my arrival in Marseilles I ripped out the notes, stuffed them in my pockets and made my way to the Marseilles dockland and the Seamen's Home.

Caskie and I were talking in the little lobby of the Home when two burly men walked in wearing the hallmarks of the French plain-clothes detective. My heart went *boum*. The Padre and I went on talking quietly. One of the detectives produced a police card and said: 'We are looking for an Englishman named Blank; we have reason to believe you are hiding him here.'

The Padre's innocent blue eyes looked pained. 'Hadn't you better look round the place?' he asked. 'The only men here have their papers in order, you'll find; they are refugees.'

'What's in there?' queried one of the detectives, pointing to a door.

'My bedroom', answered the Padre. The detectives grunted, but did not go in. They walked round the common room and then went away. The Padre and I went on talking.

'I'd like a receipt for this money', I said, 'and then I think I'd better be off in case they come back.'

'Come in here a minute', said the Padre.

I followed him into the bedroom. He walked over to a desk in front of the window. There was a screen on my right, but no

141

sign of a bed. In a moment I heard something moving behind the screen.

'Do you want a cup of tea?' asked the Padre. I thought he was asking me, but an English voice from behind the screen said: 'Yes, I would like a cup o' tea, please.'

I am afraid I jumped. The Padre turned round and said to me: 'That's only the man they were looking for. He was asleep on my bed.'

Chapter V

As IMPORTANT as it was that I should take money to the Reverend Donald Caskie in order to finance the escape route of British soldiers from the Fort St Jean, the second part of my Marseilles mission was, it seemed to me, of equal importance. Towards the end of 1940 Monsieur Pierre Baudouin, the Vichy Government's Minister for Foreign Affairs, told a press conference of foreign journalists in Vichy that the Churchill Government was starving French pregnant mothers, massacring young children and murdering French war wounded. This statement was reinforced by Marshal Pétain who, on New Year's Eve, spoke on the radio and said: 'We shall be hungry'; then he went on to blame the alleged British blockade of France. The Marshal's statement in conjunction with that of his Minister for Foreign Affairs caused a big wave of anti-British sentiments in unoccupied France. The B.B.C. put out a statement that the Germans were requisitioning eighty per cent of French foodstuffs. The Vichy Government, at the instance of the Wiesbaden Armistice Commission, officially denied the British statement. My job was to make an objective report and to see that it reached London.

The B.B.C. statement was incorrect in as much as neither

the Germans nor the Italians 'requisitioned' anything; by agreement with Vichy they had what was called 'priority of purchase', which gave them the right to take anything and to 'pay' with bonds to be redeemed 'after the war'.

In Marseilles the Germans had a commission sixty strong at the Hotel Louvre et Paix, while the Italians had a slightly smaller commission at the Hotel Splendide. The local newspapers were not allowed to make mention of the presence of the Germans and Italians, but newspapermen were informed that they were there to 'control the traffic in the port of Marseilles'. Some of the Germans 'purchased' splendid villas on the Corniche. When the villas were being purchased, the Germans went to the Town Hall and demanded to see the official assessment of values. The chief of the section instructed one of his assistants, a Monsieur Stolf, who spoke German, to help out the Germans. On the following day, when Monsieur Stolf was in attendance, one of the German officers said to Monsieur Stolf: 'Your name is not very French.'

Monsieur Stolf replied: 'I'm an Alsatian.'

'Then', said the officer, 'you speak German.'

'But only at home', answered the Alsatian.

The next day when Monsieur Stolf went to his office he found on his desk a note saying that his chief wished to see him at once. The chief said: 'I understand there was a certain incident yesterday, between you and the Germans. As your friend I shake your hand, but as your chief I must tell you that my instructions are to dismiss you immediately.'

In Marseilles at that time I found there were two shipping newspapers, *Le Sémaphore* and *Le Bulletin Maritime et Commercial* still appearing daily; moreover, *Le Petit Provençal* ran a shipping column daily. Perusal of the papers gave a picture very different from the one offered by '*les gens de Vichy*'.

The famous Compagnie Générale Transatlantique advertised five monthly sailings of its express liners from Marseilles to Algiers; two to Oran; one to Bône and Philleville; one to Bizert. The *Transport Maritime* advertised sailings to Dakar;

the Ybarra line of Seville had two monthly sailings for South America; other ships were sailing for New York and Phila-delphia, Greece and Egypt. So much for that part of the alleged 'British blockade'. But more astonishing things were in store when, disguised as a down-at-heel Frenchman, I tramped round the docks.

With the knowledge that no fewer than seventy-two ships were expected to dock in Marseilles in the near future, I found twenty thousand live sheep being landed from Algiers; there were innumerable sides of frozen beef from the Argen-tine and thousands and thousands of barrels of Algerian wine. There were piled-up crates of dried figs and dates; there were bales of cotton and legs of lamb; plenty of everything, but France was most certainly not getting very much of it. As Marshal Pétain said, France would be hungry; France was already hungry and became much hungrier—starving, in fact; but was that the fault of the 'British blockade' or of the Germans and Italians who, with the complicity of the Vichy Government, 'starved French pregnant mothers, massacred young children and murdered the French war wounded'? I returned to Antibes well satisfied with my visit to Marseilles, but almost immediately I was the subject of a violent personal attack.

On January 15th I received a message from Kennard telling me to pick up at a certain house some plans of a new German secret airfield, in a forest of all places. I was to take the plans to Kennard's house in Cannes, where Colonel C. would take them with him when he set out for England. The omnibus service between Antibes and Cannes was uncertain, so I arranged to stay the night at Kennard's. I waited a long time for the omnibus that started from Nice, but as it did not come I decided to walk the eight miles, knowing how important it was to get the plans away; I had them with me in a small attaché case along with my pyjamas and shaving tackle. I arrived at dinner time. Colonel C. had not shown up. We ate alone and after dinner inspected the plans; we could not understand the queer-looking runways, but thought perhaps that was for aerial camouflage purposes. I asked permission to have a bath, a great luxury; in my Antibes rooms there was a bathroom but no hot water. I went upstairs, undressed, and had a long, lingering hot bath. I returned to my bedroom and opened the door; the window was open and the cretonne curtains were blowing about madly. As I noticed that, I felt a violent blow on the head.

When I recovered consciousness I was lying on my face at the foot of the bed. I felt very sick. I tried to move, but found that my forehead was sticking to the parquet floor. I pushed my head back with a jerk, and then I saw that it had been lying in a small pool of blood. As I had entered the room I had switched on the light; it was still on. I groped my way to the side of the bed where I had put my watch before I went to the bathroom; the blood began to run from my forehead into my eyes. I dipped a towel in cold water and washed away the blood. I then looked at my watch; it was four-thirty a.m. I must have been lying on the floor for about five hours. I tied the towel round my head and went to bed and to sleep. At eight-thirty the manservant brought me a cup of tea; he told me how bad I looked and said he would fetch Sir Coleridge. When Kennard came and heard what I had to tell him he looked very worried, but he said he had had a message from the Colonel to say he would be coming about ten.

'The papers are over there, in my attaché case', I said. Kennard opened the case. The papers had gone. I have no explanation.

During the next month nothing of any great moment occurred in my sector, but in February I received a first-rate report on events in Rennes and Paris. A Frenchman who was the French representative of a British insurance company, Monsieur Z., had obtained permission from the Germans to cross into unoccupied France 'to visit his children in Antibes'; he had no children.

Z. was a French officer of reserve who crossed to England at the time of Dunkirk and was back in France the same day. He spoke some German and was used by the Germans as an interpreter at their headquarters in Rennes. He put on an act, making himself appear half-witted. The German headquarters were in the Town Hall, where they had a large-scale map of London; after each raid on the British capital they stuck flags on the places they claimed to have bombed and destroyed. I obtained the first information that General Milch's headquarters had been transferred to the Hotel Normandie at Deauville; as a result of my report that hotel, the Luftwaffe headquarters, was bombed by the R.A.F.

Z. gave a report on the German preparations for the invasion of Britain. In the French Channel ports the Germans had hundreds of flat-bottomed barges with a wooden handrail down the middle; German soldiers were packed into them like sardines. The barges were towed out to sea for manoeuvres, but they were so badly built that the soldiers panicked; whole strings of barges turned turtle; the soldiers, weighed down with heavy equipment, were drowned in their thousands.

Z.'s report on the work of British Intelligence in occupied France was astounding; it outdid anything told in espionage fiction stories. Z. had special reports on work in the Dieppe area, where the Germans became scared of one another because of what had happened. For instance, for more than a week a British Intelligence man had passed as a German officer, in correct uniform, and was a member of a local officers' mess. One of the officers had a birthday; before he vanished, the British officer ordered a birthday cake from a local pastry-cook's and left instructions to have the cake delivered on the appropriate day, together with a note of thanks for the mess hospitality accorded to a British Intelligence officer.

Z. reported on the mutinies among the German troops quartered in Lille. A German major arrived in Lille to attend the funeral of his son, a second lieutenant killed in the mutiny; it was from the major that Z. obtained the story. The troubles started because German troops were not granted Paris leave. On account of the mutinies, only two of the Paris gates were open to traffic; the others were barricaded. In Lille and Rouen the German divisional commanders ordered the mayors to have more women brought into the brothels reserved for German troops. In the Channel Islands there was also more unrest among the German troops. At St Peter Port the divisional commander rented two houses to be run as brothels. Forty women were brought from the mainland. They made so much money that they opened banking accounts with the local branch of a British bank that remained open during the occupation. Every Thursday morning they went to the bank to pay money into their accounts.

In Paris, through which Z. had passed on his way south, the students were playing jokes with the occupying authorities. When the news came of the first Italian reverses in North Africa, the students began wearing a piece of crêpe surrounded by macaroni in their buttonholes. The Germans thought that very funny, but they were less amused when some student stole a Wehrmacht plate from a German car and stuck it on the backside of a donkey, which they solemnly paraded round the boulevards.

Another student joke played on the Germans was a parody of their behaviour. It seemed that they went clinking into cafés, hanging up their leather belts from which were suspended bayonets, dirks and so forth. The students tied string round their middles and on it hung bicycle pumps and any old iron that made a noise, and those they hung up in the cafés. But another would-be joke had a tragic ending.

A fishing rod in French is *une gaule*. The students organised processions; at the head of each a student marched carrying two fishing rods. Every now and then the procession halted while the students shouted in unison: '*Vive!*' while the youth at the head held up two fishings rods, so it went: '*Vive deux gaules!*' ('*Vive de Gaulle*'). The Germans took action; there were arrests and shootings.

147

In the early summer of 1941 the anti-British slogans along the Riviera multiplied. On the walls of the English church in Nice I again saw the words, painted in white: 'Death To The English!' English hands wiped the words from the walls, but during the night they were painted on again. Across the pavements were the words: 'To The Stake With Churchill!'

Antibes and its immediate vicinity teemed with 'White Russians'; they ran restaurants; small hotels; made and sold yoghourt. When Hitler attacked Russia, the Russians went crazy. They became madly drunk on vodka, gave all-night parties and began packing up to return to Russia. Hitler was the toast of the coast. Then one night I heard a police van stop outside my dwelling. I thought they had come for me, but it was for the Russians next-door who ran the restaurant, the Château Fleuri. The Vichy Government had ordered a round-up of the Russians. They left the women but took the men to the barracks in Antibes for those arrested in that neighbourhood. From the restaurant next-door they took a man away in an ambulance; he had been bed-ridden for three years. But it was my turn next.

Sunday, July 6th, I was trying to send a cable to London, to the Editor of the *Daily Mail*. It had to be passed by the local police commissioner; I had to wait two hours. Part of the time I spent studying the marble 'Scroll of Honour' in the police station lobby. Most of the names inscribed in gold were those of British people who had donated sums of money to local charities; now they were to be rounded up like cattle, torn from their homes and sent into the interior. That is what Monsieur Reynard, the commissaire de police, had to tell me, and he added: 'We are coming to get you.'

When I reported at the police station to be questioned I was asked: 'Have you ever been in prison?'

I answered: 'No, have you?' At first I was given a list of departments where I would be allowed to reside. One of them was the Haute Savoie, which marches with the Franco-Swiss frontier, and, I thought I might be able to cross into Switzerland but when I opted for the Haute Savoie I was told I could not go there. I was told I would have to go to live in the Isère, so I chose Grenoble. Late at night on July 16th I arrived there, and a new set of adventures began.

Chapter VI

A FEW DAYS AFTER my arrival in Grenoble I came into conflict with the police; although the incident was not grave it was, nevertheless, a warning of what was in store.

On the Place Grenette, the centre of the city, is the large Hotel Moderne with a café that has a terrace on the Place. I was sitting on the terrace of the café one evening with a friend; I was saying how much better it was there than in Antibes. I had to go inside to satisfy a call of nature. Coming out again I saw some of the British ex-officers of the first war who ran the Nice post of the British Legion; they, too, had been exiled to Grenoble. I stopped for a moment to have a word with them, when in marched a gang of uniformed and plain-clothed police. The band that had been playing ceased in the middle of a bar; the loud buzz of conversations died away. The police began shouting; nobody to move; everyone to show their papers. I was kept standing there for two hours. One of the British officers tried to curry favour with the gendarmes, but they just looked at his papers, shrugged and said contemptuously: 'Oh, un anglais!' When I returned to the terrace my friend told me that half a dozen men had been taken away in a police van.

I was ordered not to travel more than eight miles from Grenoble without a permit, but I wanted to get to Lyons to see the American Vice-Consul, George Whittinghill, who was in charge of British interests. There were by then a number of

British subjects in Grenoble, men and women who had been rounded up in various parts of unoccupied France and exiled in this university city. But when they were heard talking English on the streets they were insulted, yet the legend that all British people were *milords* died hard, because waiters in cafés would sidle up and whisper that they could obtain various Black Market goods. When I applied for a permit to go to Lyons I was treated like a convicted pickpocket: 'Take off your hat! Stand over there!' But I got my permit. When I went to draw my first tobacco ration, forty grammes every ten days, pipe tobacco that consisted of dried dung, chopped wood and a minimum of *caporal*, I noticed a huge stock of Woodbines being doled out as the cigarette ration. They were French loot from Dunkirk.

In order to pay my fare by omnibus from Grenoble to Lyons I lived for days on stale bread and tomatoes; I was in a pretty weak state when I arrived in Lyons and saw Whittinghill. It was my intention to ask him if I could obtain a French exit visa and Spanish and Portuguese transit visas; alternatively, was it possible for him to arrange for me to receive £12 per month of my own money? Whittinghill told me he was a former newspaperman; he had been on the staff of the Chicago *Daily News*. He told me casually he had heard of me; I thought he meant as a newspaperman, but a bright light lit for me when he told me he was in the British service. Late that August night we met again, with others. There was Vera Leigh, to whose memory there is a tablet in the English church at Maison-Lafitte; the tablet says she was 'foully murdered by the Nazis', and she was, at Naziweiler, after being tortured. I had known her father, a racehorse trainer named Eugene Leigh, at Maison-Lafitte. Vera was his natural daughter, a pretty girl, engaged to a young Swiss who was at this time in his own country. They were to have married after the war, because Vera was 'too busy' now. She was a milliner employed by 'Rose Valois', the famous Paris milliners in the rue Royale. She was bi-lingual in English and French and had quite voluntarily linked up with other people in what came to be known as the Resistance Movement, but Vera was not one of those who sought publicity or who acquired glamour; there were indeed a number of heroes and heroines like her; she and they and some others had neither fame nor glory. Vera Leigh stayed on in Paris at her job even after the Germans entered Paris. Then she went to Lyons, but did not like it there so she went back to Paris and her job. Then she heard the Germans were looking for English people, so she again escaped from Paris, returned to Lyons and began the dangerous missions that ended in her death. I met other members of the band in Lyons. There was a man from St Nazaire who does not want his name mentioned; when the Germans reached St Nazaire he left—and went to Paris, from whence he brought back very valuable information. Then there was O'Neil from the Imperial War Graves base at Arras, an Irishman with a sister in a local convent. He, too, secured valuable information. But the time has come, I think, to write what I have long wanted to write, some facts about this thing called the Resistance.

From first to last, there were never more than fifteen thousand people *inside France* engaged in the Resistance, but once the war ended, hundreds of thousands made fictitious claims. The Resistance Movement so-called should be divided into three sections: firstly, those who were in France when war broke out and who stayed there as long as possible, and, in the case of Sir Coleridge Kennard and the Reverend Donald Caskie, stayed there all the time and were arrested, sent to Frèsnes, the political prison, and then interned in St Denis. How the Reverend Caskie came by the nickname he claims, 'The Tartan Pimpernel', I really do not know; it strikes me as being very inappropriate. He did fine work, but the things sometimes claimed on his behalf are fantastic. In Grenoble, as a result of the strain under which he had been living, his nerves were badly affected, which perhaps accounts for the inaccuracies of what he himself wrote.

The second section of the Resistance was that run by the

Free French from London; they did magnificent work. The third section was that run by the London War Office, which often, to me, appeared to be in direct competition with the Free French. This section was magnificently paid; they had money belts weighed down heavily. Reading some of their books is like reading a gourmet's tour of the Black Market restaurants of unoccupied France. While we were starving, those gentlemen, according to their books, were living on the fat of a France we never even knew existed. Wing-Commander F. Yeo-Thomas, who himself played a prominent part in the Resistance movement and who authored *The White Rabbit*, deplored the fact that never has sufficient tribute been paid to what certain French people inside France did to help the Allied cause. The Wing-Commander wrote me: 'All the books I have read deal with agents sent out by Colonel Buckmaster, none refer to agents sent to France by the Free French. Hence the legend that all achievements in France were attained thanks to Colonel Buckmaster; whereas the Free French, in reality, had a much more important and numerous organisation. Unfortunately, when it came to supplying the Free French, they were in general only given the leavings after Buckmaster had been served. I tried to make that clear in *The White Rabbit*. There were Resistance movements in France, as you yourself know, long before the British agents came over, and they did sterling work.'

Incidentally, it is a fact well worth recording now that it was only after Wing-Commander Yeo-Thomas had an interview with Mr Churchill, as he was at that time, that greater facilities were granted to the French.

On my first trip to Lyons I secured a mass of information; in political intelligence work no item of information is too small. There was the question of soap. In Lyons at this time (August, 1941) people used to go to a church and buy a candle, really a thin taper, for twenty centimes. They took the tapers home with them and then picked laurel leaves. They took the leaves, melted the church tapers, and from the mixture made small cakes of soap. The public libraries were besieged by people looking up formulas for making soap. Laundries refused to wash linen unless one provided one's own soap. The German Armistice Delegation in Lyons was housed in the Carlton Hotel on the Place Bellecour; a notice stuck on the glass doors instructed the people of Lyons not to importune members of the Delegation: a notice that spoke volumes about their willingness to collaborate. Lyons, once the world-famed centre of the silk trade, now had two million shuttles idle, but the good people of Lyons were being offered *ersatz* material made from broken glass, or fish bones, mixed with boiled-down hens' feathers.

In Lyons and in nearby Valence the Italians had their own Armistice Commissions, mostly engaged in 'exchanging' goods with the French, who invariably came off worst. The Germans in exchange for some promised wheat secured 190,000 head of cattle; 600,000 sheep; 600,000 pigs and calves; 36,000 tons of household oil; 100,000 tons of salt; 60,000 tons of fresh vegetables; 8,000 tons of cheese. After the French began their deliveries they asked for the wheat, only to be told that 'transport conditions prevent deliveries for the present'.

When I returned to Grenoble I found a notice had been stuck up over the reception office desk in the hall of the Hotel Moderne; it said: 'No Jews Admitted'. Incidentally, the Hotel Moderne was also exhibiting a notice outside saying it was an R.A.C.-recommended hotel. German missions passing through Grenoble always stayed at the Hotel Moderne, so any Jew who happened to be staying there was turned out. Among those was an English Jew from Paris, a Mr Nathan, who was there with his Belgian wife and two daughters. As he was leaving he said to the reception clerk: 'When my brother-in-law arrives next week, tell him you kicked me out, will you?'

'What name, Monsieur?'

'General Buat.' General Buat, formerly Governor of Paris, was married to Mr Nathan's sister.

I was now living at the Hotel d'Angleterre where there were

a number of British people who were daily insulted by the proprietor or by some of the French guests, one of whom used to shout every time she passed a British person: 'Intern all the British in concentration camps!' I suggested to the proprietor that he should rename his hotel the Hotel d'Allemagne. But some of the British people now in Grenoble were certainly not behaving well. A number had found the means to bribe the police to allow them to return to the Riviera; others bribed doctors to give them false health certificates. Worst of all, a number wrote personally to Pétain seeking favours. Some of the Riviera refugees seemed well supplied with money and I wondered how that could be; then I found out. Across the garden from my hotel was the Café Excelsior, with a large back room where every morning the German and Austrian refugees who had managed to reach Grenoble ran a sort of stock exchange, where the open-dated cheques of some British residents in France were bought and sold as if they were stocks and shares. One could hear buyers and sellers of the cheques of Captain B. or Colonel P. quoting their prices and thus one knew the varying state of credit of those who had no scruples about selling Britain short.

There was a regular tariff for letters smuggled across the line of demarcation, and although I saw only three British newspapers in fourteen months, there were ways and means of keeping in touch with the news. I contacted a French journalist named Lombard who had served with de Gaulle in the first war and did not have a very high opinion of him. Lombard was on the staff of *Le Petit Dauphinois*, published in Grenoble. I asked him if the staff believed the stuff they published; he said half the staff was pro-German, or pro-collaboration, as he put it, and half was not.

I received reports about the British internees' camp at St Denis, on the north side of Paris, where about two thousand British males were in barrack buildings two hundred years old. Subsequently, my St Denis report has been edited and amplified by Alex Potter, a British journalist who has lived a lifetime in Paris and who was interned in St Denis. Potter says: 'The majority of us were there for nearly four years; after a year or two most of us got on each other's nerves. I saw no cruelty or brutality by Germans, but they missed a chance of showing us how a camp should or could be organised.

'The Germans gave us a starvation diet; if the only food that entered the camp had come from the Germans, many of us would have died; but the Germans did allow food to come in. We receive a Red Cross parcel every week; wives and friends brought food; vegetables and a few other things could be bought in a canteen, and for a while we even had a restaurant. Men who arrived from the German prison camps gained anything from six to twenty pounds in weight in two months. I gained seven pounds in weight in the camp, but I lost it all in Paris during the first three months of Liberation!

'The Germans solved the clothing problem in St Denis camp by ignoring it; they did not give us a stitch; they employed some of our tailors and shoemakers to work for them. Besides the food parcels, the Red Cross gave us some clothing, and fifty cigarettes a week. Then, to our surprise, we were allowed to buy the French ration of eighty to a hundred cigarettes a month.

'We were allowed visits, half an hour a fortnight. If one were a camp worker one could have a visitor for half an hour a week, but I *was* able to see my two children grow.

'We had three hundred francs a month pocket-money; this came through the British authorities, who also made allowances to our dependants. It was a lazy, futile, boring but safe existence; no bomb ever fell nearer than a mile and a half away, although at the end of the war, when there was street fighting around St Denis, German mortar fire hit our building twice. Even when our internment was over, the fighting continued; one internee was killed; three were wounded.

'Our biggest problem was the smuggling of a little Red Cross food to our wives and children. If an internee had any spare food, and the Red Cross parcels arrived so regularly that almost everyone had a reserve, the temptation to slide something across the table on visiting days was almost irresistible. The penalty for discovery by one of the German sentries who walked up and down the hut was the suspension of visits for one, two or three months. Giving a bar of chocolate to a child meant a two months' suspension of visits. At first some of the sentries shut their eyes to the smuggling, but then Major Mobuis, and after him Hauptmann Gilles, said they would stamp out the smuggling; we were searched before entering the visit huts. For a week or two, women visitors suspected of receiving packets of food were searched by a German female nurse. Some of the women hid food under their skirts or in their blouses. One woman put two square tins of preserved meat under her blouse. An English-speaking German who saw her leaving the camp said: "I've seen some strange-looking women, but this is the first one I've seen with square breasts."

'One German anti-smuggling sentry we named "Charlie the Chocolate Chaser". He seemed to smell a bar of chocolate at fifty yards. He would take it from the children and punish their fathers. Another sort of German sentry was he who wept at the sight of the children's gratitude for the chocolate we gave.

'News flowed into the camp. Visitors told us what the B.B.C. told them. Frenchwomen in nearby houses signalled or shouted items of news. The R.A.F. dropped leaflets which were smuggled into the camp. We had one or two hidden wireless sets. The maker of the first set tried it out by blanketing himself and the set in his bunk; he sweated for an hour, but all he heard was: "There was no football in England today".

'We had football, cricket, tennis, cards, bowls, billiards, a library, a few theatrical shows, concerts, and a cinema that mostly showed German films which received "fruity" applause.

'During the time I was interned about twenty internees escaped.'

Englishwomen and elderly British men were interned at Vittel, but I had no information about them until later when I made my way out of France.

Chapter VII

MY DREARY LIFE continued. Very soon after I was back in
Grenoble from Lyons, I had the police in my room a little after
six one morning. During the night they had erected wooden
barricades in the streets. There had been a monster round-up;
there had been rumours of an anti-Vichy plot. It was bitterly
cold, and heavy snow had fallen during the night. The police
looked at my papers and asked why I was where I was. I told
them it was because I had nowhere else to go. I heard mutters
of: 'Concentration camp'.

I thought I would have one more try to get exit visas and
transit visas, so once again I plotted to go to Lyons and back
without being caught. The journey each way took about
three hours; I travelled by bus, but I had to work out my
journey like a game of chess. I planned to go on the first
omnibus which left Grenoble at six-thirty a.m., and to return
on the last omnibus, which left Lyons at six-thirty p.m.; thus
both journeys would be made in the dark and the cold, so there
was less chance of the gendarmes stopping the bus and asking
people for their identity papers, but to increase my own safety,
I booked a seat right at the back of the omnibus, near the
emergency exit. I did that because I reckoned that if the gendarmes stopped the omnibus, they would hail the driver, and
enter the vehicle by the door next to the driver; that would
allow me a chance of jumping out through the emergency
door. The snag was to be sure of getting a seat on the last
omnibus returning to Grenoble. I thought that if I stayed over-
night, I might be caught, unless Mr Whittinghill could hide
me in his flat, but I did not want to ask him to do that. In the
event, it turned out all right, because I booked a seat, also next
to the door, just as soon as I arrived in Lyons.

As soon as I left the omnibus, I jumped on a tram, from the
Place Bellecour to the Quai Général Sarail; that is where the
British Consulate was. I stayed there until lunchtime. Then I
went to a small nearby café and sat right at the back and took

an *ersatz* coffee, and a sandwich I had brought with me; I remained there until the Consulate re-opened. Then I went back and stayed until it was dark. Then I walked the streets until the time the omnibus was due to leave, jumping aboard at the last moment. Whittinghill had warned me to keep clear of the cafés on the Place Bellecour; he said that was where the police were most active. He also advised me to go into hiding because, although I had not been stopped either going or coming, it was highly probable that I was under police observation.

So for three days I went into hiding up in the mountains at St Nizier. I was practically forced to go because one of the police in Grenoble warned me that there was going to be another round-up of Englishmen, and that he had seen my name on the list. I had made a friend of this man, because one day when I was at the police headquarters I had noticed a man wearing an English golden sovereign on his watch-chain. I talked to him and asked him where he had obtained the English piece of money; he told me that it had been given to him by an English soldier in the first war. This man also warned me that most of the police in Grenoble were anti-British.

I went to a small hotel right away from anywhere. There was an electric train that climbed up from Grenoble twice a day, but it could not always make the grade, because of the snow. There was a Captain Barley and his wife living in St Nizier. Both of them were expert skiers, and he had skied down to Grenoble to tell me that the coast was clear and it would be safe for me to go up to St Nizier. He used to ski down and take the electric train back.

In Grenoble things had been going very badly for me. My room in the hotel was costing me two-thirds of my income; there was no heat at all. I had a choice of freezing in a cheaper hotel and perhaps being able to eat, or to get a little heat, but that meant existing on a starvation diet. I was very weak indeed, as I had been living on a very awful-looking grey bread, and a sort of liquid cheese I discovered: it was a local product called *conquelt*; once I believe it was a delectable mixture of white wine, oil and white cheese, but now it was just anything at all. However, one could spread it on the awful-looking bread and it gave one the illusion of eating. Up at St Nizier I tasted both butter and milk, neither of which I had known for many months. I felt somewhat better when I returned to Grenoble. I had made the acquaintance of the late Georges Lafourcade, who then held the Chair of English Literature in Grenoble University. He had held the French Chair in Edinburgh and in Boston, Massachusetts. He was the author of a biography of Arnold Bennett. During the war Lafourcade had been a member of the French Mission with the British Army. Like many another of his kind, he was very critical and very bitter but, nevertheless, he arranged for me to enter the University and attend lectures on political economy. Lafourcade took me to see René David, one of the law professors, who had just recently escaped from a prison camp in Germany. David's English was as impeccable as Lafourcade's; he had been educated at Cambridge, and now, as I saw him sitting smoking a pipe, wearing his college blazer, he looked no older than an undergraduate. David spoke perfect German. He was much more friendlily disposed to the British than Lafourcade. David told me he was five months preparing his escape from the German prison camp. He passed as a German; in the train he fainted, and when he recovered consciousness he was afraid that he might have spoken French, but it was all right. He reached Nancy, so he thought he would call on the Rector of the University. David related his escape from Germany. The Rector heard him out, and said: 'Young man, as you come from Germany, perhaps you can explain our French Government!'

David told me that in Nancy they turned the official pictures of Pétain face to the wall. He learned from a woman who came from Verdun that the wives of the French prisoners of war in Germany were living with the German soldiers in that city of great heroic memory. The woman said that the insolence of the Germans when there was an air-raid alarm was unbelievable. They turned the French out of the air-raid shelters and used them themselves, and would not allow the French to use the German-built shelters.

The struggle now in Grenoble was how to keep warm and also how to obtain something to eat. For some time I had been eating at a small students' restaurant kept by an Italian woman. The waiter was a medical student. The place was so packed that it was difficult to use a knife and fork, because people stood between the tables, waiting for a seat to pounce on. But I had to abandon the restaurant. They served a thick soup, thickened with—I have no idea what it was; sawdust, maybe. Many a time I lifted pieces of newspaper out of my soup, but one could not complain, otherwise one would not be served again. However, when I fished out a piece of cotton waste from the soup I thought it time to leave for good. I found that I had fallen practically to the level of a dog. I was so hungry that it hurt. Sometimes I found myself crying from sheer weakness. Then I went down with influenza, because I had queued up for three hours in a biting east wind in order to get a little imitation jam. Then one day I found some potatoes, which tasted marvellous after a long diet of boiled *chardons*, a species of giant nettle. The students at the University were for the most part pro-de Gaulle. I often found '*Vive de Gaulle*' cut in the woodwork of the desks.

At this time much was being made of the so-called Riom trial. Blum and Daladier were on trial, among others, and they sought to throw all the responsibility for the fall of France on to General Gamelin. Gamelin said it was all the fault of the politicians. However, the Germans soon made the French put an end to the Riom farce.

The mass shootings of French people in occupied territory had their repercussions in Grenoble. The British were blamed for everything. And, as I have already had cause to remark, the behaviour of some of the British was very bad indeed. There was a little under-sized man, who had a wife and daughter in England, but he had been living at Perpignan. He spoke fluent German, and was well educated, but during the Spanish Civil War the French had arrested him for his pro-German remarks. In Grenoble he talked pro-German propaganda to all and sundry, and one day he said to me: 'Well, when are we going to haul down the flag?' It was impossible to hit him; for one thing he was too small, and for another, I was too weak. But I did know that he had obtained a sum of fifty pounds from Whittinghill by fraud. He pretended that he was to undergo an operation, which was entirely fictitious. I advised Whittinghill of the facts, and Whittinghill made the man refund the money. At this time I heard from Whittinghill that it was impossible to obtain Spanish and Portugese visas for me. I had sent in several applications to Vichy for the French exit permit but I never obtained an answer. Then, while I was thinking of making yet another visit to Lyons, in came the police once again.

It was the end of December, 1941, when the police visited the hotel where I was staying. They came knocking on every door, and asking if there was a foreigner inside. When I went downstairs there were more police in the lobby, with one sitting at a table. Everyone was asked questions. When I was questioned I put my passport on the table and said: 'All the answers are inside here.' The policeman copied out everything, and then asked me what my religion was. I suppose I was feeling facetious, so I told him I was a Plymouth Brother. That seemed to puzzle him. Then he said to me: 'What race are you?' I told him quietly and politely that I was a member of the human race. People standing round began to giggle. The policeman glared at me, and closed my passport with a bang, but I was not stopped when I went out.

In the third week of January, 1942, I went down with a bad bout of malaria. I now ran into trouble with the proprietor of the hotel, because he said that unless I stopped listening to the B.B.C. on my wireless, he would have my wireless set confiscated. If I had been better and stronger I would have moved out of the hotel. I particularly remember the night of January 18th, because that was the first time, so far as I was aware, that the R.A.F. passed over Grenoble on their way to bomb Milan.

By now I had made certain local connections; Kennard and Caskie and Grounsell were all living in and around Grenoble. There were some secret meetings, and discussions of ways and means. Practically our only friends at this time were the students and the Jews. Then I went again to Lyons, but all to no purpose, although I did have a bad fright on my way back. It was about nine-thirty p.m., and of course, pitch dark; I had no idea where we were. I suppose I must have been dozing, when the jerk of the omnibus stopping woke me. I looked up and saw a gendarme getting into the bus. There was only one. He looked cheerful. I dropped the book I had been reading purposely, and leaned down, so that I could watch the gendarme at the same time, with my hand on the door handle, and jump out if I had to. If there are two gendarmes, I said to myself, I will make a jump for it. I looked unshaven, and typical of French of that kind. Nobody could guess that I was English, and if they thought I was French, possibly nobody would give me away. It all happened in far less time than it takes to tell the story. The gendarme pulled the door to after him, and sat down in an empty seat near the driver, who slipped into gear, and the omnibus moved forward in the inky darkness. He was just getting a lift home!

It was in February that I saw a man about whom I had been warned. His name was Neumann, and he was known to be a German subject and an *agent provocateur*. Caskie had informed me that the Gestapo were employing him, a renegade Jew, and that he would be trying to get into touch with me. Often I had been dodging suspects. I refused to see strangers who called on me at the hotel. Sometimes I was stopped in the street by men who asked me how they could get to England. It was possible that some of them were genuine cases, but one could not take chances. Then one day I was sitting in the little hotel salon, when the door opened and a young man walked in and sat himself down beside me on the sofa. He said in English: 'You are Mr Greenwall?' I nodded. Then he went on to say that he knew I had been with a certain London national newspaper. I guessed at once that this was the redoubtable Neumann. I asked him, and he said his name was Neumann. Then he went on to tell me that he had worked for the *Daily Express* in Berlin. I asked for the address of the office, and he gave me the correct one. Then I asked him for whom he worked. He named three British journalists. But, the first one he named had left Berlin many years before; the second one had left the newspaper many years previously, and the third one had been killed in Shanghai certainly a number of years previously. I asked him if he had any papers. He produced a German passport which I took out of his hand. The first page was obliterated with a large 'J' in red ink. I looked at the visas; they were Swiss, Italian, Chinese, Bolivian and various others, but there were only indications of the Swiss visa having been used. I pointed out that the passport had been cancelled a long time ago. He agreed, but said that unless he got help he would have to work for the Germans. I said to him: 'Are the Germans now recruiting German Jews?' He said to me: 'Look here; I've got something I want you to get to England at once.' I asked him what it was and he said it was the 'plans for the German Spring offensive'. The same old story trotted out once more; the same story that the mysterious woman had tried to plant on Sir Coleridge Kennard in Cannes, as I have related. I told him that he had better get out at once. As he stood up, he dropped a sealed envelope on my lap. I noticed it was already stamped. He said to me: 'Please have that registered and mail it for me.' I asked him why he did not mail it himself, and he answered that he had no money. Then he turned on his heels and ran out of the hotel. I had to make up my mind pretty quickly. I said to myself that the cost of registration was only about a franc, so that if he had money for a stamp it was strange he didn't have enough money to register the letter. The letter was bulky and addressed to Lyons.

Then it occurred to me that if one registers a letter in France one has to sign the yellow registration form, which is naturally a record of one's signature. I dropped the stamped addressed envelope into the letter-box outside the hotel, and thought no more of Neumann, but that he was a clumsy *agent provocateur*, until a couple of days later, when I was told to come down to the lobby because a postman wanted a signature from me. It was a registered letter, I thought. No, it was a postal order for three francs. I asked the postman's permission to look at it. It was from Neumann; his signature was on it as the sender. I gave it back to the postman and said I refused it, but why this man, or those who sent him to me, wanted my signature, was something I never knew.

Chapter VIII

ACCORDING TO MY diary, between February 5th and March 7th, 1942, I ate nine meals. The nearest to a good meal was on Sunday, February 15th, when I had a tiny piece of roast beef, not more than a mouthful, some chopped carrots and cabbage, and some *ersatz* jam, which was made from turnips, sweetened with what was called *jus de raisin*, which was black and stained the teeth. For breakfast I had two slices of the so-called bread, which I had to toast in order to be able to swallow it, and a cup of imitation tea, drunk without sugar or milk. I could have had rationed sugar, but I do not take sugar in tea; in any case, there was no milk. When I could procure some of the so-called liquid cheese, I spread it on the toast. For lunch I had some of the liquid cheese on some of the bread; sometimes I was able to get my ration of wine.

March 15th, one of the servants came to my room to say there were two detectives downstairs who wanted to see me at once. I asked if they were seeing anybody else and I was told that they were not. When I went downstairs the hotel clerk said the detectives were in the proprietor's private sitting-room. I went in. One of the men, of early middle-age, was sitting with a notebook in front of him; the other, who was fat, was slumped over the table. I opened the conversation and asked what they wanted with me. The more alert one gave me his card and I saw that his name was Broner. I told him that I had an American journalist friend in London of that name. The detective said he had an uncle in America. Then I looked at the inert, fat detective; he was dozing. Broner tilted his elbow and in pantomime pretended to drink. I asked with enforced jocularity what I could do for them.

'We've come from Vichy', said Broner. 'Your dossier has arrived from Paris.'

I said: '*Alors?*'

Broner looked at his notebook and began to rattle off some biographical notes. Then he looked up at me and asked: 'When did you join the British Intelligence Service?'

I told him that that was perfect nonsense; I was sent to Grenoble in 'forced residence' and I was waiting for an exit visa to leave France. The fat detective then showed signs of life; he got up, and said to Broner: 'I'll see you later', and went out. I began to try to talk to Broner, and asked him if he had ever been in England. He said he had not; he said he was of Alsatian origin. I asked him if he liked the Germans. He shook his head. Then I asked him why he worked for them. He did not answer. Then we talked about Alsace for a full fifteen minutes, and I thought everything was going well, but suddenly Broner asked once again: 'When did you join the British Intelligence Service?'

I said to him: 'You people have got that on your mind. I am a journalist; you've seen that in my dossier; what good would I be to the British Intelligence Service?'

Then Broner asked what I did while I was in Grenoble. I told him that I waited and I worked. He asked me at what I worked, and I told him I was writing a novel, and I was also writing articles for the New York *Nation*, and the *Baltimore Sun*. He wrote that down like so many others before him. Then he said: 'I want a list of the books you have written, and the names of the publishers.'

I said that if he would wait a few moments I would go up to my room and get him a list. It was very fortunate that I did say this.

I went out of the room, and just as I was crossing the lobby to go up in the lift, I heard from the reception desk somebody calling me in a whisper. It was the woman clerk, a Mademoiselle Mureaux. I tiptoed over to her.

'Better look out', she said. 'They're after you. Seriously, this time. He', she nodded towards the sitting-room, 'asked me if you received many letters and telegrams and visitors, and who your visitors are; I shouldn't be surprised if it was the *patron* (the proprietor of the hotel) who denounced you. You had better get out of here.'

I nodded my thanks, and went upstairs and prepared a list of my books and went back to the sitting-room.

'Thank you', said Broner, rising and putting the list in his pocket.

'Going to be in Grenoble long?' I enquired casually.

Just as casually he answered: 'Oh, I shall be around.'

'Good', I said. 'I'll be seeing you then; we must have a drink on one of the alcohol days.' One could drink alcohol three days a week.

'Sure', said Broner, and left me.

Mademoiselle Mureaux handed me a slip of paper. I looked at it and read: '11 rue Bizanet.'

'Go there,' she said, 'and say you have come from me; you'll be all right there; they are all friendly people in that district. Get a tram from the church; you'll be all right; you'll see; they'll let you have a room, and maybe you needn't register; you'll be all right', she nodded. I thanked her, and went off.

The rue Bizanet was right on the edge of the town, in a bend of the river Isère; the district is known as the Isle Vert. The street was slippery with thick, unmelted snow. The Alps, snow-covered, seemed very close. The houses were just bungalows. Number eleven was a wooden chalet set back from the road. I could see nobody. Then a woman came out of the house next door. I showed her the piece of paper. She was an Italian. She showed me a room on the ground floor of the chalet. It was a tiny room with a divan bed. I had to pay one hundred and fifty francs a month for the room, and twenty-five francs a month for the Italian *concierge*, Madame Arletti, to make my bed and clean up every day. I asked who my neighbours were, and I was told that they were quite all right; those below me, that is to say in the basement, were refugees from 'up there'—she meant occupied territory. Then in the house there were two French sergeants and their wives. I moved in the following day.

Now I had a terrible cough. I had seen a doctor, who said I had a crack in my lung, and I ought to go and live in a less damp place than Grenoble, which seemed rather poor advice. I sat down as soon as I moved into the rue Bizanet, and wrote to a former colleague of mine on *The Times*, the late Henry Daniels, who was then Press Attaché in Berne. I asked him if he could possibly get me a Swiss visa. Then I wrote to Whittinghill, and begged him once again to try and use his influence with the French to reply to my requests for an exit visa. I told him I had written to Berne.

By the end of March I received a letter from Daniels saying that he could obtain a Swiss visa for me, but then matters became complicated, because Whittinghill himself went to Berne and, when he returned, he broke his journey in Grenoble in order to see some of us, including myself, and he told me that I would soon be needed.

My daughter, Joan Gilman, was now in Grenoble with me.

She was staying in a flat kept by a Monsieur and Madame Bank. Monsieur Bank, who was subsequently shot, said that he had been the editor of a newspaper in Morocco, and that he had been wounded in the first war and in the second war too. He said he was at Dunkirk. All those statements I believed to be true. His wife was very much of a mystery. I learned later that she had a police record for theft and petty larceny. However, I did not know this at the time, and I arranged to have an evening meal with them: soup and a vegetable, for which I was to pay eleven francs; that was all that I had to eat at the time, except once or twice a week. It was now a very long time since I had even seen milk or butter. I kept on having to make new holes in my belt to draw it tighter, and my collars were too big, and my clothes hung on me in a ridiculous manner. I found that when I shaved, my skin was like that of an 'Indiarubber Man' whom I once saw in a freak show; when I pulled out the flesh, it stayed pulled out. I coughed and coughed, and sometimes spat up a gout of blood, which was rather frightening.

Madame Arletti proved something of a humbug. Three or four nights a week when I came back to my room I found it just as I had left it in the morning; I had to climb into a frowsy bed and cough myself to a shattering wreck. I also see noted in my diary that at the beginning of April I spent several days trying to buy a button. At this time I looked so awful when I looked at my face in the mirror that I almost frightened myself. I had absolutely no strength at all. I had to walk so slowly that it was quite painful. I remember waiting two months to get a pair of shoes soled and heeled, and on one occasion when I went to see whether they were ready, the cobbler picked up the shoes and hurled them at me.

Then I received a cryptic message to say that I had to be in Cannes on April 12th. I was told the hotel at which I was to stay; it was a small hotel opposite the station. At this time Pierre Laval was trying to get Georges Bonnet to join him in the Vichy Government, but Bonnet remained in Paris and refused to leave. They had tried to assassinate Laval at Versailles, and one morning in the Jardin Victor Hugo in Grenoble, somebody had painted up during the night: '*Vive Collette*'. Collette was a young man who shot at and wounded Laval. Early the next morning municipal employees painted out the notice.

To read the '*Journal Officiel*', the Government daily publication, was the only way to obtain any news at all. Here one read the decrees published in Vichy, and there were many decrees showing how the Germans were gradually obtaining control of France. All the big businesses and industries were turned into Franco-German monopolies; on the board of directors were both French and Germans, but there were always two Germans to one Frenchman.

The reason I had to go to Cannes was because an R.A.F. flight, which was going to bomb Milan, was to bomb the Rhône factory at La Bocca, a suburb of Cannes. In the Rhône factory they manufactured Gnome motors for aeroplanes. I was provided with an electric torch, and I was to signal positions to the flight. An incident that occurred when I travelled to Cannes by omnibus on April 10th was illustrative of the situation of British people at this time. Captain Barley and his wife, to whom I have already referred in this narrative, were travelling in the same omnibus, as they had received permission to visit their property at Cagnes. Sitting across the aisle from me was a hefty-looking blonde young woman; one could guess she was a Scandinavian. A tall young Frenchman got into the omnibus just before it started; he began to move the hand luggage in the net just above the woman's head. He shouted in a loud voice: '*Les français d'abord!*' which means, of course: 'The French first.' Nobody took any notice. Then the Frenchman again said the same thing, and he added in French: 'The English have no rights here.'

The woman snapped at him: 'I am not English!'

'*Et avec ça!*' sneered the Frenchman.

The woman leaned over and gave the Frenchman a sharp

blow to the muscles of his right arm. He muttered something, but I did not catch what he said. The woman rose, and swung her right hand to the Frenchman's face. He staggered back. Then a little man, who had been sitting next to the Scandinavian woman said, in quite a strange accent: 'That will teach you to insult women.'

The gallant Frenchman, having been defeated by the blonde woman, and seeing that the interrupter was only half his size, turned on him: 'Monsieur, with your accent so slightly French, I advise you to shut up.'

The little fellow rose, staggered in the aisle pushing out his stomach in front of him, and shouted: '*Monsieur, je vous enmerde* —is that French enough for you?' The Frenchman subsided in his seat, muttering that he would call the police when we reached Digne, where the omnibus was to stop for an hour. Just before Digne, the Frenchman said to the Scandinavian woman: 'Madame, will you accord me a few moments?'

'No!'

'Madame, I apologise.' There was silence.

'Madame, I apologise, but it was you who struck me.'

There was raucous laughter in the omnibus. When we resumed our journey to Cannes, the gallant young Frenchman was not among those present.

The next day in Cannes I learned that Captain Barley and his wife had been arrested in Nice and had been held all night. Their lawyer, an English lawyer, who had not been rounded up, was also arrested. He had been dining that night at Cap Ferrat with Lady Hatfield, when the police telephoned from Nice to say his presence was requested immediately. He went to the police station and was taken inside and put under arrest. He did not know that his clients were in an adjacent room. It seemed that Captain Barley had been slightly merry in Ruhl's Bar in the morning, and had been boasting how easy it was for him to obtain money; the Italian barman, who was a police informer, denounced him. The police arrested Barley and his wife as they were cycling along the Promenade des Anglais, going back to Cagnes. It seemed that everything was cleared up satisfactorily, But not so for the planned bombing of the Rhône factory.

I was on duty at the time and place indicated to me by Kennard, but nothing happened. I waited and I waited. Then I went back to my hotel and to bed. At two-thirty a.m. I was woken by police whistles, and by the noise of bursting bombs. I slipped on some clothes and rushed out. A few small bombs had dropped in the sea near the Casino, and a few incendiaries in the Avenue nearby, but nothing dropped near the factory. I could only hope that the B.B.C. would not announce that we had bombed the factory, because there had been another fiasco in the previous year, when we were supposed to have bombed the Kuhlmann factory at Arras. The B.B.C. announced that the R.A.F. had left the factory in flames. In point of fact, not a bomb fell within four hundred yards of the target. That sort of thing, which I suppose was inevitable, did a tremendous lot of harm.

Chapter IX

THERE WERE SOME quaint English people in Grenoble. There was a widow who had been an Edwardian chorus girl; until she was forcibly removed from Nice she had lived there in reasonable comfort; now all she cared about was how to get back; the war was 'an awful bore'. When I tramped around questing for food I used to meet her similarly employed. Invariably she would greet me with the query: 'What's the news?' and just as inevitably I would tell her what I had heard on my hidden wireless. Always she dismissed this with an impatient: 'I don't mean that; I mean, what's the news about getting back to the Riviera?' The lady lived platonically with an unfrocked English clergyman whom she always called 'Jane'. The selfishness of some of the Englishwomen was sickening. One woman said to me when there were strong rumours of the British being put into concentration camps: 'But what shall I do for my chocolates and flowers?'—when only the small minority who were selling British cheques in order to purchase Black Market food had more than the bare necessities of food.

Donald Caskie in his book does not relate his queer experiences with British people. He had a small stock of tinned butter and tinned jam he held for cases of almost complete starvation. An Englishwoman wrote him and said she was so hungry; could he call on Thursday and bring her some food? He called on the Wednesday and found her, so he told me, sitting down to a hefty piece of cheese, bread and butter—all luxury articles in those days. A Miss D., formerly in the theatre, also wrote and said she was destitute. Caskie sent an old Englishwoman, also formerly of the theatre, who sometimes gave him a hand. The lady helper found Miss D. lying in a corner of an hotel bedroom; all the furniture had been removed; she was lying on a bed of straw. 'Ah, still in the theatre, I see, Miss D.,' was her comment. Subsequently Miss D. obtained an exit visa and money to go to England; she had two dogs, but she was warned that she could not take her dogs into England. When she arrived in Lisbon the skeletons of two dogs were found in her luggage.

Caskie was kind to the British people stranded in Grenoble. Sometimes he would go round leaving tins of jam and butter on the deserving, but many had near heart failure when he knocked on their doors, they feared it was the police come to fetch them away to a concentration camp.

'Qui est la?' they would enquire quaveringly; Caskie would answer reassuringly: 'Le pasteur anglais!' Why he had to say it in French I never knew. Before he was finally arrested and taken to Frèsnes prison he had the Gestapo in his hotel room to cross-question him. That was in 1942, just after he told me that the Chanoine of Grenoble had told him that some French students had been tortured because they would not 'give away' what they knew about Resistance developments in the neighbourhood.

The youths had their fingers crushed in a vice; one boy— Caskie said he had seen him—had four fingers of his right hand so crushed that the bones were broken. The Chanoine wrote a letter of protest to the Prefect, but that is all that happened.

By this time Kennard, Grounsell, Caskie and I were active again, but we were hampered in many ways. The R.A.F. were dropping explosives, arms and various things, including chocolate; but they did not always, by no means always, fall into the right hands; too often those who found them sold them. We were also hampered by two dreadful British liars: one, an ex-Army officer who had been secretary of a club in Italy, told anybody who would listen to him that he was a member of 'British Intelligence'; the French were only too eager to listen to tales of his imaginary exploits, but he was the cause of great embarrassment. Another was the elderly man I have already mentioned, he who called himself a colonel, whereas he was an absconding bookmaker from Penang; his great story was of imaginary British planes that used to come to fetch him away to Britain—and bring him back! He even had the audacity to try and tell Caskie that story.

The French were running their own resistance in the Isère department, entirely unconnected with the British. One of my jobs was to take messages to a man named Jean Bruller; I am not sure that I ever saw him face to face, but he became world-famous as an author, under his Resistance name of Vercors. The centre of the French Resistance in those parts was in the tunnels known as the Petits Goulets, which are surrounded by steep mountain walls; there were waterfalls, grottos and springs, and pine trees everywhere. Other places were Uriage, where Kennard was actually living, and Seyssinet, Sassenage and St Nizier. Many useful things were planned and plotted in those places and, what was more to the point, a number of them, acts of sabotage, were put into effect. But my personal job was mainly the collecting of information concerning French activities, particularly with regard to collaboration between the French and the Germans.

In April, 1942, I met the American journalist, Dosch-Fleurot. He had been to Vichy, where he heard that the Allies were going to land in North Africa. I thought it a silly story. Then I went to Lyons once again, to hand on information, without a permit naturally; on my way back I was nearly caught.

Vichy had refused my exit visa unless I agreed to leave my daughter, Joan Gilman, behind in France as a hostage against my 'good behaviour'. Joan was born in France, and although she was British by birth and travelled on a British passport, in France she was regarded as a French subject and had French identity papers. Naturally, I would not accept a visa under the conditions imposed. Whittinghill could do nothing to help me; he himself was now an object of suspicion and was preparing to return to the United States.

I left Grenoble early that morning; I saw Whittinghill and then stayed hidden until it was time to return to Grenoble. I had my seat near the emergency exit of the omnibus and was reading a Penguin copy of *Death Comes for the Archbishop*. I fell into a doze. I suppose it was the stopping of the omnibus that woke me. I opened my eyes and saw two gendarmes in the front of the omnibus, looking at the passengers' identity papers. I said to the man opposite me: 'I'm just going outside for a moment.' He nodded. I lowered the doorhandle slowly and jumped into the road; I pushed the door to behind me, without closing it. I doubled round the back of the omnibus and walked quickly past the near side; the omnibus had stopped at the entrance to a small village. I walked on in the direction the omnibus would be following; my first idea was to board the omnibus again further on, but then I thought it would be better to stay the night in the village; if the gendarmes looked for the missing passenger they would not, I thought, search the village that night. Then I discovered I had left my book behind somewhere: in the omnibus, or had I dropped it when I jumped out? That worried me; an English book would arouse suspicion.

I walked on in the pitch darkness; then I found a small café-restaurant and went in. I knew that there was nothing British about me except my accent, and I could do nothing about that. There was nobody in the café but a young and pretty waitress; I asked her if I could have a glass of beer and maybe some bread and some cheese. She asked if I had bread and cheese ration tickets; I told her I had. I gave her a ten-franc note and said: 'I've walked a long way and am very tired; I have no luggage because I meant to be in St Marcellin tonight. Could I have a room? I'll pay for it now.'

'I'll ask the *patronne*', she said; she was back in a minute. 'The room will be twenty francs.' I gave her the money.

'What about your beer and cheese?' she asked.

'Could I have that in my room? I'm terribly tired.' I tried a pathetic smile. As I went up the dark rickety stairs I heard the omnibus rumble by.

When the girl came to my room with a black japanned tray with my beer, cheese and bread, I thought I would try and bluff her.

'Can you let me have the registration form now?' I asked.

'Won't it do in the morning?' she queried.

I simulated a drowsy yawn; 'Oh yes; all right, that will do.' I knew I could creep out before dawn and wait for the omnibus from Lyons. The cheese was as dry as a bone and full of worms, so I drank my beer, ate part of the grey-looking bread, and went to sleep.

Spring came to Grenoble; the hills around my little room were white and pink with fruit blossoms, but it seemed as if Nature was laughing at me; I was starving and often light-headed. I felt so ill and weak that I scarcely went out, but when I did I found that the people in the immediate neighbourhood were friendly and pro-Ally. Sometimes in the dusk, young fellows would ride close to me on their bicycles and whistle softly or under their breath hum 'The British Grenadiers', which proved they had been listening to the B.B.C. One evening when I was coming back from the town, walking along the riverside, three policemen on bicycles came up silently behind me, surrounded me and asked for my papers. One read out my identity card while another took notes. I remarked that the one who read pronounced my name English fashion. I said to him: 'You have a good English accent!' He answered: 'I speak English.' I suggested to the three of them that we should go somewhere and drink a glass of beer. One answered that they were still on duty. The one who said he spoke English looked at his watch and said it was nearly time he went off duty; he would accept. He wheeled his bicycle to a café. We sat down and talked for two hours. He was, he said, from Marseilles. We talked all round the war but not directly of it. When we parted we shook hands and he said in French: *'Bon courage.'* I needed it.

Towards the end of June I stayed in my room for three days. For a long time I had been living on nothing but a few potatoes I cooked for myself, plus my ration of so-called macaroni. On the night of the third day I was wakened by a tapping on the iron shutter of my window. It was Madame Arletti. She whispered: 'Get dressed quickly; there is a police van at the other end of the street.' I scrambled into my clothes and opened the door. It was a lovely moonlight night but very cold.

'You had better get away', said Madame Arletti; 'if they come for you I'll say you are in Lyons.' I crammed pyjamas and shaving things into my haversack and covered my bed over to look as if it had not been slept in. Then I locked the door, gave Madame the key, and dropped about three feet over the side of the garden staircase, climbed a low wall, crossed a garden, hoping that my blundering feet would not disturb the occupants of the villa, climbed another wall and reached a little street that gave on to the river at my end of the rue Bizanet. I walked along the river bank, fearing all the time I might start dogs barking either by my awful cough or my footsteps on the stony path. I looked at my watch; it was nearly four. I knew that the first tram for the mountains left Grenoble at five twenty-five. But I had to cross Grenoble and feared I might meet a policeman, so I sat on the bank of the river behind a clump of osiers and waited for it to get light; then I could walk the streets as if I were a workman.

Then for three nights I slept in a cowshed at Charvet, sharing my dormitory with six soft-eyed, light-brown cows!

I alighted from the tram at a place known as the Pas de Curé and wandered around until eleven. There was a grotto and I wondered whether I could sleep there, but I went to a local inn known as Wandel and there for the first time in months and months I drank a glass of milk and ate some bread and butter; it was like a golden dream come true. But there was no room at that inn, so I still had to find somewhere to sleep.

I came upon a stone farmhouse on the edge of a small plateau; there was a marvellous view; Mont Blanc showed up like a monster wedding cake trimmed with pink icing. An old couple kept the farm, but like all French farmers at that time, they would not sell anything for paper francs; they would barter eggs, say, for cigarettes or pipe tobacco; a goose could be obtained, perhaps, for a pair of shoes. But I had nothing to offer; however, I found that the old lady needed wrapping paper, and in my haversack I had some old newspapers; these I bartered for two eggs. Then I discovered that the old lady in her youth had been a *midinette* in the rue de la Paix and liked to talk about Paris, so I talked about Paris and coaxed a little cheese made from sour milk, but still I had nowhere to sleep. When I suggested a room, they shook their heads. Then the old man went out to the cowshed and I followed him. I gave him a pipeful of my precious tobacco. At the end of the six-stall shed was a pile of sweet-smelling hay beneath a barred window. I suggested humbly that I might sleep there. The old man was doubtful; we went back to the farm kitchen, where I repeated my request. The old lady laughed when I said I would help on the farm, but she said yes, and the old man said yes, too. So that night and for the following two nights I slept in the hay, thinking that if Christ was born in a manger, a poor sinner like myself might well sleep in one. No more fear of raps on the door; no more mad nightmares; I slept undisturbed but for the occasional clumping of my fellow lodgers, the six soft-eyed cows.

When I returned to Grenoble I was startled by the sound of air-raid sirens; it was to be a regular thing, every Thursday. Why, I never knew.

Time passed so slowly. Then came July. Lombard, the local journalist I have already mentioned, told me that there was to be a landing in North Africa; he said that a report from Vichy affirmed that all British and American subjects were to be sent to concentration camps as soon as it happened. General Giraud had escaped from a German prison camp; Lombard had a remarkable story about him.

According to Lombard, the Germans insisted that Giraud had given his parole that he would not attempt escape; therefore restriction had been relaxed; but, said the Germans, as he had broken his parole, Giraud must be returned to them. Pétain, however, as a fellow-soldier, refused to surrender Giraud. Then it was agreed that Giraud, Laval, Otto Abetz and Admiral Darlan should meet on the line of demarcation between occupied and unoccupied France.

The meeting took place; there was a discussion about the war; Giraud insisted that the Germans could not possibly win. After further discussion, Darlan turned to Laval and said, textually: 'Well, what did I tell you; I said they were licked!' Later, Giraud, no doubt with the complicity of Pétain, got away to North Africa; later still, Darlan followed him and was assassinated.

On July 7th there was another knock on my iron shutter, late at night. It was my daughter, Joan Gilman, who called to say that a detective had visited the place where she was living; she was out; he had left a message to say she must call immediately at the police station. When she called the Inspector said to her: 'Look here; no nonsense; we know who you are. You've got to do a job for us. We know you speak English, French and German (her knowledge of German was slight). The German Labour Recruiting Bureau in Grenoble has told the Prefect he wants two secretaries and we are to provide them. You will have to report to us every day what goes on in the German office.' Joan was dumbfounded.

She said: 'But I am a British subject.'

'That doesn't matter', answered the Inspector. 'We have bitter pills to swallow and you must swallow one, too.' Joan asked for time to think it over.

'There is no time', said the Inspector. 'The Chef de Cabinet of the Prefect wants to see you at eleven tomorrow morning.'

Joan called attention to her name and said the Germans would realise it was not a French one.

I had to think quickly. I told Joan to keep the appointment, see the Chef de Cabinet and point out how dangerous it would be for the Prefect if the Germans found out that he had placed a British subject in their office.

The eleven o'clock appointment was kept. The Chef de Cabinet was not impressed with her story; he said the Prefect wanted to see her at four p.m. and she must report at three forty-five. I passed hours of despair. The German office was opposite the station. I kept it under observation. I counted the number of people who went in; there were not more than a dozen, and most of them were Algerians.

Joan returned to the Préfecture at the indicated hour. The Chef de Cabinet said: 'I mentioned the matter to the Prefect and he agrees with you about the name, therefore we are not nominating you.'

Reprieved, but for how long? I wondered.

Chapter X

MY CONTACTS WITH unoccupied France were haphazard, but still, from time to time, I did have news of my cottage in Chantilly. I heard from the mayor, who wrote that the cottage was *externally* intact; the italics were his; he could not vouch for the contents of the house. Then came a puzzle. I did not learn until after the war was over that my house had been pillaged by the good people of Chantilly, before the arrival of the Germans, but through the faithful service of a former *concierge* of a block of flats in which I lived before renting the cottage, I received a cabin trunk full of clothes. The kind woman obtained the trunk from the loft and packed and despatched it. I was surprised to find among my clothes about a dozen neatly-typed sheets in German: fragments of a play! I stored the trunk of clothes in the flat occupied by Monsieur and Madame Bank: he who was subsequently shot, and she who had a police record. Perhaps it was not surprising that all my clothes were stolen.

I made a formal complaint to the Grenoble police, but obtained no satisfaction. After I escaped from France I learned that in April, 1943, the two police officers I saw, Commissioner Rémy and Chief Inspector Berdeseau, were themselves arrested. The allegations against them were that they obtained goods from Grenoble shopkeepers by torture. They called on the shopkeepers and told them they had to report to the police station; there, in a hidden room, they tortured the unfortunate people until they signed a paper 'confessing' imaginary crimes. According to further statements, the two police officers obtained a million francs' worth of goods in that way.

On the few occasions when I was able to eat in a restaurant, I found the food was terrible indeed. There would be a soup plate full of warm water in which a cabbage had been boiled, followed by a plateful of cabbage, just plain boiled. Near where I lived were some allotments from which I occasionally stole a few potatoes and onions. Food, or rather the lack of it, was the one topic of conversation; if one passed people talking in the street and overheard the talk as one passed by, it was always food that they were discussing. A woman who tracked a cabbage was regarded either as a genius or a slut who was undoubtedly sleeping with the greengrocer.

I used to get reports from Vichy. The most popular man there was Pétain, and the most unpopular man was Laval. Pétain, now he was eighty-five, used to rise very early and go early to bed; he ate heartily and consumed a bottle of claret at each meal. He adored his wife, whom he had known since she was five, and he called her '*Mon Maître*'. His face and hair were snow-white. He was the prototype of the old man the French love: *un petit vieux bien propre*—'a nice clean old gentleman'.

When Pétain met Hitler at Montoire, the question of the French colonies was discussed. Hitler told Pétain that he proposed to send an army of technicians to the French colonies 'to put them on a sound basis'; France would be allowed 'prestige of possession', but France would have to carry the financial burden of the German administration.

Pétain answered saying that among the thousands of French unemployed there were plenty of men capable of developing the French colonies, therefore the employment of German technicians was not necessary. Hitler did not press the matter.

The censorship of the French press prevented the public knowing about anything inimical to France until after the event. For instance, the conflict in Indo-China was not reported until Pétain had surrendered bases to Japan and her then satellite Siam; then it was announced that there had been a 'peaceful settlement'. When Britain occupied Syria to prevent the Germans taking it, that was presented as a British act of aggression *against France*!

In Grenoble, which could be taken to mean a city representing the whole of unoccupied France, excepting Lyons, there was very little opposition to German domination. In cinemas there was whistling, equivalent to English booing, during the compulsory showing of German newsreels. As a consequence, the house lights were turned up during the showing of those newsreels, which meant that the whistling ceased. French newsreels, particularly those featuring Pétain, were received with frantic applause. The Germans issued a decree prohibiting the showing of British or American films 'dubbed' in French; prior to that decree I saw the original version of *Mr Smith Goes to Washington*; it was advertised as *'parlant American'*. To such lengths went that artificially created Anglophobia. But it should not be forgotten.

The Germans prohibited the French publishing any translation of an English work written since 1886; as a consequence, there was a rush for translations of such American authors as Faulkner, Steinbeck and Hemingway, who escaped the ban, of course. There was a great shortage of paper; once I spent two days searching for a packet of envelopes, but Vichy found no paper shortage when it came to publishing propaganda vilifying Britain. In July, 1942, there appeared a large poster depicting a bulldog wearing a Union Jack cap, its paws on a globe map showing how Britain had stolen French colonial possessions: Canada, Egypt, Malta, Syria, Madagascar. About this time, British prestige reached a very low ebb. Apropos of the fall of Tobruk, Captain Barley, a former Hussar officer, said to me: 'It has no importance, it never belonged to us'; the late Captain Kruse, a former director of the *Continental Daily Mail*, remarked to me: 'What's the odds if Egypt does go? It was never of any use to us.' A former French Consul told me: 'The English are no good; their soldiers have no courage.'

In August I did what was practically my last job of obtaining reports and getting them to London. Caskie in his book relates a story about Commander Prior, but he tells only a part of the real story. Maybe he did not learn the full story; here it is:

In the Dieppe raid was a Commander Prior who was taken prisoner. He escaped and reached Grenoble, where he was very ill; with forged papers we took him to the Grenoble hospital which was on the edge of the Isle Vert, where I was living. The Commander drafted a report on the raid; it was, in effect, a blistering criticism of Earl Mountbatten. Later I learned that it was alleged that the preliminary bombardment by naval vessels was terribly inefficient, with the result, when the invaders attempted to scale the Dieppe cliffs, they came up against barbed-wire entanglements that they had been told were destroyed. What happened to the report once it reached London I do not of course know. Under Caskie's direction the Commander reached Britain, and was later elected to Parliament.

My daughter Joan Gilman went to Lyons, travelling as a French girl, with her French identity card. She went to see Whittinghill because once again a French detective called on her; she was out; he said he had come to check up on her identity papers; she was to report to the police as soon as she received the message. She did, but learned nothing at the police station. Nevertheless, the visit of the detective had sinister implications, because the French were now calling up for service all girls who could not prove they were working more than thirty hours a week; that meant that the girls were liable to be sent to Germany. Joan had been teaching; she had plenty of work in the winter months, but little in the summer; certainly not thirty hours a week. In Lyons Joan spent the night in the flat of an absent British agent known only as 'Harry'. There were a number of British agents now in and out of Lyons, but I would so much like Captain Peter Churchill to know that none of them known to me ever partook of those wonderful Black Market meals he was so fortunate to find in starving France and which he describes at some length in his book. Whittinghill, now on the verge of departure, said he would urge his chief, the American Consul-General in Lyons, Marshal Vance, to use his influence with the American Ambassador at Vichy, Admiral Leahy, to persuade the Vichy Government to recognise Joan's British passport, but her mission to Lyons failed, because shortly after her return to Grenoble Vance telegraphed that the matter was hopeless, and that he could do nothing.

Matters were now rushing to a crisis. In the middle of August Grenoble overflowed with rumours. First of all, all French Jews were to be arrested; a camp was being prepared in the outskirts of Grenoble. Then Whittinghill came to Grenoble to settle up some matters. He and I were sitting in the little Café de la Poste, on the Place Grenette. Donald Caskie had discovered that one could get a drink there on non-alcoholic days. I always felt there was something queer about the place, but I never knew what it was. The *patron* was a big, husky brute and definitely anti-British; his wife and their very beautiful daughter appeared to be extremely pro-Ally. Yet, when Liberation came, the French liberators shot the wife.

Whittinghill and I were having a farewell drink. The waiter came to us and addressing Whittinghill said: 'Your friend wants you down the back there.' Whittinghill looked surprised, but he got up and found it was Madame who wanted him.

'Tell your friend', she said, meaning me, 'that he must get away at once; the police are after him.' Whittinghill asked her how she knew; she answered evasively that detectives had 'just' told her that all the British were to be rounded up that night; Whittinghill said to her: 'Tell the detectives that the American Consul would like a word with them.' Madame looked down the café and said: 'Oh, they must have gone!' What it was all about we never knew; there was no round-up that night.

I destroyed all my Dieppe notes in case the police came; apart from Commander Prior, there were three Canadian Rangers who had been taken prisoner in the raid, and who had escaped. The camp at Fort St Jean had been transferred to another, outside Lyons. Caskie had been able to bribe the Camp Commandant, who had facilitated the escapes, but the Commandant was now changed, so escapes were exceedingly difficult; whichever way one turned there were increasing difficulties.

There was now a regular tariff for people crossing the line of demarcation. A clandestine crossing in August, 1942, cost two thousand francs, split fifty-fifty between the Franco-German guards. Those who could not pay risked being shot dead by either the French or the Germans. I met some of those who had succeeded in crossing, both men and women. They crawled across on their bellies, in the darkness of the night, taking hours to crawl a few yards. At this time it was two years since I had seen an English language newspaper; I depended on my wireless for the real news of the world and listened to every B.B.C. newscast I could. Sometimes I listened to Vichy and one night I heard Pierre Laval say, textually: 'I wish with all my heart for a German victory.'

The time came to say goodbye to George Whittinghill; he was leaving for Lisbon to take the Clipper to fly to New York. Before he left he said to me: 'There is just one chance for your daughter; I've just remembered that we have a man named Bernard working in the Ministry of the Interior at Vichy. Tell her to try and see him and ask him to procure a French passport for her; if she can obtain that, she will be able to leave the country in safety.'

Just after Whittinghill left I became very ill indeed; once again I lay in bed for three days. There I lay, listening to the wireless when, once again, and for the last time as it proved, I heard tapping on my iron shutter. Here they are then, I thought; this must be the end. I can fight no more. I crawled over to the window.

'Who's there?' I croaked.

'Hello, this is Dosch; open up!'

It was Dosch-Fleurot, the American journalist; Joan had brought him along to me. I was so low-spirited and weak and so glad to see him that I burst into tears. Joan went back to her room; Dosch-Fleurot stayed with me until two in the morning. He had broken his journey from Cannes to Berne to see me. He had been in Vichy, where he had learned from the American Embassy that the Allies were going to land in North Africa within the next few weeks.

'They'll take you out and shoot you then', he said. 'You won't stand a dog's chance; you must try and get away. If they catch you, you won't be any worse off.'

'And what about you?' I asked.

'I shall be all right', he answered; he was then a man in his sixties; 'I'll stay two weeks in Berne and as soon as I get back I'll try to get to North Africa; If I can't, then I'll join you in Lisbon, but be sure to go.'

Dosch-Fleurot was arrested as soon as the Allies landed in North Africa; with other Americans, mostly diplomats, he was interned in Bavaria. In 1944 he did join me in Lisbon, when there was an exchange of civilian prisoners. Dosch-Fleurot died in Paris in 1947, when he was packing—to go to North Africa.

When Dosch-Fleurot left me, I did some thinking. I saw Joan, and arranged with her to go to Vichy. Here is her report on what happened to her there:

'When I left Grenoble to go to Vichy, the train was absolutely packed; people were sitting on the steps of the railway carriages, and it was with the greatest difficulty that I managed to get into the train. Not only was every compartment full but people were standing in every compartment, and the corridors were crowded with standing people. I could not move along the corridor, but opposite the entrance to the carriage was the toilet. The door was open, and that too was crowded with passengers. There was somebody sitting on the toilet seat; there was a man sitting on the wash handbasin. There was a man sitting on the floor and there was another one standing. I pushed my way in and stood. After standing I suppose for an hour or more, the man who was sitting on the washhand basin said to me: "Mademoiselle, would you like to take my seat for a while?", and this I did.

'It was late in the evening when I got to Vichy, too late to go and see my contact. In those days one could not obtain a room in a hotel without sending them money when one applied for a booking, and this I had done. I reached the hotel and found that half of it had been requisitioned by the Ministry of Education. The hotel clerk gave me a room and I was taken to it, but I found it was full of luggage and a man's clothes. I called the clerk's attention to this, and was told not to bother about it; it would be quite all right. I got some food, and I went to bed. In the middle of the night there was a commotion, which woke me up, of course; there was a man in the room; he was making a great fuss. It appeared that he was a schoolteacher employed by the Ministry of Education, and this was his room. In order to make a little money on the side, as the man was absent, the hotel had rented his room twice. I refused to leave the room because I said I had booked a room and I had paid in advance, and unless they were prepared to give me another room, I was going to stay where I was. Eventually everything quietened down and the man agreed to share a colleague's room somewhere further along the corridor, so I was able to go back to bed.

'The next morning I went to the Ministry of the Interior to see my contact. He was a Monsieur Bernard. I had to wait hours. There I sat, waiting and waiting. I went out about lunchtime and then I came back and I was told it was too late to see Monsieur Bernard that day and I was to come back the next day. I managed to get another room in the hotel and I returned to the Ministry the next day, and was able to talk freely. Evidently Mr George Whittinghill had advised Monsieur Bernard that I was coming, and he knew what it was all about; he asked me only a few questions. I came provided with a photograph, and he said that I was to go back to Grenoble and very shortly I would obtain a French passport, which would enable me to leave the country, but I had to hide my British passport and also my French identity card.

'What impressed me most about Vichy at the time was that everything was terribly overcrowded. This of course was partly accounted for by the fact that it was the capital of unoccupied France, but it was difficult to walk about the streets. The thermal baths were still working. The shops were much better provided with goods than the shops in Grenoble and Lyons.

'In the restaurants, the food was better; everything of course was rationed, but there was a better choice of food. The return journey was pretty bad and not very different from the outward journey.'

About a fortnight later Joan obtained her French passport, which meant that unless she was held up on the French frontier, she could eventually join me in Lisbon. She had strict instructions to hide her British passport. It was agreed that I should get away at once and that she should follow me a week later. Incidentally, that French passport was most useful, and not only to Joan. When she reached Lisbon she went to work for a certain service that smuggled people out of France, and it was her passport, suitably altered, that served to save the life of another person.

So, after more than half my life spent in France, I left the country I loved so much and which I had tried to serve; but, as I said in the beginning, when France fell, I fell, too.